Hello, Fiona."

The deep male voice resonated through her body, causing the cup to tremble in her hands.

Her back still as wood, Fiona turned. "Michael Shaughnessy. What are you doing here? What is it you want?"

"Fiona, I—" He glanced down at the dingy floor, the cluttered countertops, the crystal-clear front window.

A tiny brown bird with a twig in its beak fluttered from the ground to the top of the window. Michael blinked at the sight, thinking how gracious God was to care for the sparrows, and he knew that, though he certainly did not deserve it, God would provide for him as well.

His mind went to the verse Benny had tried to quote: *Seek and you will find.*

Then his eyes landed on the "Help Wanted" sign he'd never noticed before.

Ask and it will be given to you.

His lips tugged into a smile. "I came to apply for a job."

Palisades.
Pure Romance.

Fiction that features credible characters and
entertaining plot lines, while continuing to uphold
strong Christian values. From high adventure
to tender stories of the heart, each Palisades
Romance is an undiluted story of love,
from beginning to end!

A PALISADES CONTEMPORARY ROMANCE

Irish Rogue

Annie Jones

PALISADES

IRISH ROGUE
published by Palisades
a division of Multnomah Publishers, Inc.

and in association with the literary agency of Writer's House, Inc.,
21 W. 26th Street, New York, N.Y. 10010

© 1998 by Luanne Jones
International Standard Book Number: 1-57673-189-8

Cover illustration by Paul Bachem
Cover design by Brenda McGee

Scripture quotations are from:
The Holy Bible, New International Version (NIV) ©1973, 1984 by
International Bible Society, used by permission of
Zondervan Publishing House.

Printed in the United States of America

For information:
Multnomah Publishers, Inc.•P.O. Box 1720•Sisters, Oregon 97759

Library of Congress Cataloging-in-Publication Data
Jones, Annie.
    Irish rogue/Annie Jones.
        p.cm.
    Sequel to : Irish Eyes   ISBN 1-57673-189-8 (paper)   I. Title
PS3560.045744I76   1998
813'.54--dc21   97-30830
                                                             CIP

98 99 00 01 02 03 04 — 10 9 8 7 6 5 4 3 2 1

For all my loopy sisters: Gail, Maureen, Tina, Laura, Linda W.,
Cheryl, Bonnie, Deb, Jill, Lena, and Margo (Mango).
If I left someone out—I'm sorry!

And especially for Rhonda Gibson, Suzie Johnson, and
Patti DeGroot,
for actually looking at Irish Rogue
and telling me not to give up writing—yet!

May those who love us, love us.
And those who don't love us,
may God turn their hearts;
and if he doesn't turn their hearts,
may he turn their ankles
so we'll know them by their limping.

—IRISH BLESSING

In this you greatly rejoice, though now for a little while
you may have had to suffer grief in all kinds of trials.
These have come so that your faith—of
greater worth than gold,
which perishes even though refined by fire—
may be proved genuine and may result in praise,
glory and honor
when Jesus Christ is revealed.

1 PETER 1:6–7

Prologue

IRELAND

"Gold, gold, gold. I'm sick o' the talk of it." Fiona Riley clapped her hands over her ears and shut her eyes.

Michael Shaughnessy laughed at her dramatics and tugged gently at her wrists. The bright red curls hanging over her fingers fell away when he pulled her hands against his wool sweater. He shifted his worn tennis shoes in the damp grass to move closer to her while the brisk spring breeze whipped the full skirt of her print dress against his legs.

"All right then, darlin' girl, no more talk o' stolen gold or lost land or the wrongs done against the Shaughnessys and O'Deas these many years past." He dropped a kiss on her lips.

She responded in sweet innocence. Her eyes opened, shimmering with emotion, as he pulled away.

He brushed his thumb over her cheek. "We'll speak instead o' happier things. Have you yet chosen a date for our wedding?"

"I have not," she whispered.

"And why not?" He pulled her so close they stood heart to heart, and gazed into her honest green eyes. What Fiona found to love in such a man as he, he would never suppose to guess. But he thanked the good Lord every day for her coming to him, for her steadying influence in his tumultuous life.

She was just a bit of a thing, fine boned and fair skinned, scarcely two months shy of her nineteenth birthday. Yet she filled his arms as thoroughly as she filled his senses. He breathed in the quiet scent of her, stroked her lower lip with the tip of his thumb, and managed the faintest of smiles himself. "Don't be tellin' me you've changed your mind about marryin' me?"

"It's not *my* mind that needs changin', Michael."

"Your father is still that set against it?" He scowled and stepped away from her to lean against the gray stone wall that divided two pastures.

She kept her hands on his chest, moving with him. "If you would accept the job with the jewelry maker and stop all this talk o' regainin' the fortune taken from your family—"

"Jewelry maker." Michael spat out the words.

Fiona touched the dainty Claddagh ring that Michael had made for her. The design was an old Irish symbol of friendship, fidelity, and love—two hands holding a heart with a crown above it. "You have such a knack for the craft, as your father did before you."

He harrumphed.

"It's a gift, Michael. Your family has had it for generations, and they do the finest o' work. Your own father might well have made a better way for you in the world if he'd used his talents wisely. Don't be squanderin' your life as he has."

Poverty, pity, and a pint of ale: that was all his father had left these days. And while Michael knew full well that Fiona had not mentioned his father's downfall in a hurtful way, it still stung him to the quick to hear it.

"So I've learned to cast gold and silver into rings and brooches, to fashion charms and medals to dangle on chains," he grumbled. "'Tis no real trade, not one with a future."

"That isn't true. Anyone with a talent such as yours could do well if he fully used his skills. Everybody is sayin' so."

Michael jerked his chin up and narrowed his eyes. "And does everybody say where it is I'll be selling this jewelry I make? How I will be feedin' my family in a trade with no customers? There's no better hope for it now than my father ever had."

"At least it's an honest way to make a livin', and there's no shame in that."

He stood rigid. "There it is, isn't it?"

"What?"

"The truth, lass. You say you're sick o' the talk o' the gold my grandfather and his partner spirited away, the money rightfully his and his father's before him. But listen to yourself." He pushed his hand back through his closely cropped hair. "An *honest* way to make a livin'. No *shame* in that."

She lowered her eyes.

"Your very words tell me that you know the name o' Shaughnessy is sullied and it ever will be until I find that gold and make my rightful claim to it."

"Even if you did find it, you could never make a rightful claim to it."

"Why not? It's mine."

"It's not yours."

"If you mean I'd have to be sharin' it with the family O'Dea, well, for sure they'd have their part of it. They deserve their portion."

Fiona looked to the horizon, her lips pursed as if ready to speak but unable to do so.

"The O'Deas hold the secret of where it is buried," Michael went on, taking her by the shoulders. "But 'twas the Shaughnessys' legacy long before that, Fiona. If I could place my hands on a single one o' those gold coins, I could prove it. And I won't rest until I can do just that."

"I feared you'd say that, Michael." Her voice rasped like silk dragged across cement. She took one step back, away from his touch. "But I had to hear it straight from you to make myself accept that's how you were feelin'."

"You're not makin' sense." He huffed a hard breath.

"You're the one who's not makin' sense, Michael Shaughnessy. You say you want to marry me, then with your next breath say you can't provide for a family usin' your God-given talents. You say you want us to have a happy future together, but you're unwilling to let go of the misery of the past."

"That's your father talking," he accused. "And all the other fine, 'decent' folks of this village who wouldn't give a Shaughnessy the time o' day."

"I speak for myself, Michael." She pushed back a lock of hair that had tumbled over her cheek. "I don't care what others might say of you, as long as when we take our vows before God and man I know it's me who's first in your heart and not some foolish quest for a reward that can never be yours."

"You sound like you're askin' me to choose." He chuckled nervously even as he begged her with his eyes to deny his claim.

She exhaled slowly, her expression grave. "I am."

He felt a cold stone fall to the pit of his stomach.

"What's it to be, Michael? Me or your precious gold?"

"I can't make that choice," he whispered.

Fiona inched her chin up, blinked back the tears glistening in her eyes, and stepped away. "Then you already have."

One

CINCINNATI, OHIO

FIFTEEN YEARS LATER

God had forgiven Michael Shaughnessy. He knew it in the very core of his being, just as he knew that the people he loved most in this world, those he had hurt the deepest, might never find it in their hearts to do the same.

"You're a free man, Shaughnessy. Guess you had more than a little Irish luck going for you—this time."

"A free man." Michael shook his head at the irony of the term and at the officer's implication that he would cross the law again. Both couldn't be further from the truth. As long as the old injustice against his family remained unsettled, as long as the people he most cared for despised and feared him, he could not be free.

However, with the whole matter now out in the open as it was, he'd never again need to tread so close to the thin line between right and wrong. His cause had always been right, and he believed in it still, but his desperation to prove his claim had pushed him too far. His methods of accomplishing his goals had gone terribly wrong.

He understood that now. And with the Lord's grace, and his own humility and renewed sense of integrity, he'd do whatever it took to make sure those he'd hurt knew he understood it. He owed them that much.

Michael gave a passing nod to the man who had handed

him his belongings in a large manila envelope, then headed for the nearest restroom. In the cold, dirty, tiled room, he tore open the packet to retrieve his wallet, his wristwatch, and his gold cross on its heavy braided chain.

He slid his wallet into the back pocket of his jeans and slipped the watch on. Then he turned his attention to the cross.

He'd cast and engraved the filigreed piece himself, following the tradition of his family, who had been jewelry makers and metalsmiths for generations. It brought memories of home, family, and faith that flooded back so suddenly he had to curl the cross into his fisted hand to keep from feeling over-whelmed. He'd once had a future creating fine handcrafted jewelry if he wanted it, but he had believed then that his only real future lay in pursuit of another kind of gold.

That pursuit could now call him home to Ireland to follow the path that had consumed him for most of his life. He thought of his childhood, of the poverty he had known in his family. He thought of the scorn he'd received from others over a crime that was none of his doing. He saw the glittering eyes of his father's grubby cronies as they spoke of the time one of 'their kind' had exacted payment for ill-treatment by those who abused power. He realized how hard that life had made him, how it had shaped him into a man of single purpose and calcu-lating coldness. That man had passed away with his acceptance of Christ when he'd been a teenager, only to surface again when the lure of gold and retribution reared its head.

If the time in jail had done anything, it had given him time to think on his sins and to make peace with himself again—and with God. He would not go back to Ireland to follow the gold that was now being returned.

He'd once thought it a matter of family honor, his duty as a

Shaughnessy to reclaim the gold coins taken by greed and circumstances from both his grandfather and great-grandfather. Now that he had perpetrated his own injustice, it was his duty as a man to make amends. That was the path he must now follow.

In his mind flashed an image of Fiona Riley O'Dea and of the son that should have been his had Michael's stubborn pride not driven her to marry another. The only woman Michael would ever love had become the bride of Neal O'Dea, a man much like a brother to Michael, almost fifteen years ago. Then, a year and a half ago, she'd become a widow.

He had been on the fringes of her life for so long, always too far away to be counted kin and too close to allow his wounded heart to heal. After Neal's death, Michael had stepped in as a male influence for the boy, a shoulder to cry on. He kept his emotional distance from Fiona, unwilling to take advantage of her fragile state, but that could not protect her from the fallout when he went after the gold he'd sacrificed so much to find.

The image of Fiona as he'd last seen her, when he returned with her son, haunted him still. He would never forget the pain in her eyes that day. He saw Fiona's compelling features, her flaming red hair, the mischief that normally gleamed in her green eyes. His chest constricted at the thought of the pain he'd caused her. Regret washed over him, and something more.

He'd never known how much that petite pixie of a girl still meant to him until he had to face the fact that by his own actions, he'd lost all connection to her.

Or had he?

Slowly, he lifted the necklace to his throat, and meeting his own wary green eyes in the streaked mirror, he fastened the cross around his neck. He finger combed his dark auburn hair, then set his square jaw, threw back his shoulders, and headed through the door. For the first time in weeks, he strode with his chin high, out of the jail and into the dazzling morning sunlight.

"I cannot believe they just let him go, just let him waltz out o' jail, happy as you please. After what he did to you—to both of us."

"Mom, we've gone over this time and again." Devin O'Dea rolled his eyes in that way reserved solely for thirteen-year-olds who have suddenly realized with indisputable certainty that they have the densest parent on the face of God's green earth. "You know the laws. You know them better than most Americans born into their citizenship."

The lilt of home had faded from her son's accent, much more so than her own. To an American ear, she supposed, his words still hung heavy with a distinct brogue, especially when he was nervous or excited. But Fiona rarely heard that, and it saddened her a bit. She missed the lyrical turns of phrase that took her back, if only for an instant, to dear Ireland.

Still, Devin was an American citizen now, as was she, and there was no shame in sounding like one. She perched on the arm of Devin's chair and brushed her hand through the boy's copper-colored hair, just a shade darker than her own short curls. He'd been through so much these last few years.

The immigration from Ireland to America and the loss a year and a half ago of his beloved father and grandfather in an automobile accident would have been difficult for any child to bear. But for a sullen boy, small for his age and reclusive, with only his imagination for a companion, it had proved grueling.

A weary sadness settled over Fiona at her own loss. Her late husband, Neal, had not been perfect, far from it. His stereotypical old-world thinking made him distant and in some ways domineering over his wife and child. Too often, boisterous, hurtful arguments had filled their home instead of kind words and loving support.

She had made peace with herself and the Lord over that rocky relationship and her young widowhood. But sometimes, such as when she watched her son sink into his own cheerless world, she wished Devin had happier memories of his father. Fiona couldn't help but speculate whether Neal's death or his early influence on Devin lay at the heart of the boy's troubled spirit.

Fiona glanced down at her son. How she longed to comfort him, to reach beneath his posturing exterior and connect with the little boy who had once come so freely into her arms. She smoothed one hand down her gray slacks and said a small prayer that she could one day find the sweetness in her child again.

'Twas a prayer she found herself murmuring almost daily, apparently to no avail. Still, she had faith that God heard her plea. Faith, Fiona mused as she watched her son pretend to read a school book, had kept them going in the midst of their grief, and again when a century-old family curse had disrupted their lives.

Gold. Fiona swallowed the bitterness brought to the back of her throat by the thought of the stuff. The wanting of it, the theft of it, the hiding of it, and the years of longing after the precious metal had sullied the O'Dea and Shaughnessy names like a dark stain that could never be completely wiped clean.

Nearly one hundred years ago, her late husband's grandfather and the grandfather of Michael Shaughnessy had stolen a cache of gold coins from a greedy politician. Legend held that the coins were in reality payment due, an issue involving land and family treachery, that O'Dea and Shaughnessy had been cheated out of the gold by a man with a soul corrupted by power and greed. Many locals in their small village called the thievery justice, not avarice, and elevated the culprits to the status of heroes. Others said O'Dea and Shaughnessy had been seduced by the lust for gold, pure and simple.

On warm nights in dark pubs the story was told time and again. Behind the church after services and over the neighbors' fences on Monday mornings the tale was spread. Opinions were offered, debates raged, harsh words and sneering jests hurled, and wild, imaginative tales spun about the golden coins forever lost and about the men who supposedly knew where the pot of pilfered gold lay hidden.

But neither Michael Shaughnessy nor Neal nor Neal's brother, Cameron, knew the whereabouts of the gold. Only Fiona's father-in-law knew, or so he broadly hinted to all who would listen. And it was Colin O'Dea who brought the search for the gold to America. Three years ago, he'd moved with Neal, Fiona, and Devin to America, as Michael and Cameron had years before, and continued the search here in Cincinnati.

Whether because of the tales, the money, or a matter of family honor, both Michael and Cameron became obsessed with finding the treasure. For Cameron, it boiled down to a means of restoring the family's good name. Motivated by that desire, he became an agent of Interpol and used his skills to track the gold, as a means of penance for the ill deeds of his grandfather.

For Michael, who took the view that his grandfather was a martyr to justice and not a common thief, the quest for the gold took on a darker, even more compelling aspect. He would have his gold and his family honor, and he would not let anything or anyone deprive him of it. Fiona knew that full well from their younger days, when Michael had chosen his obsession over marriage to her.

Their personal history made his betrayal of her trust in using her son as a bargaining chip to get the gold all the more difficult to bear. She'd tried to put it behind her. She'd thought pursuing justice would help her move on. Yet when she'd concluded her interviews with the police and her discussions with Cameron, she'd come to understand that it was a legal matter, not a personal one.

"Yes, I understand that the state, as the lawyers called it, had no case against Michael without your testimony, Devin." Fiona lifted her gaze to the far wall of the apartment. "I even understand why you might feel reluctant to accuse a man you love of kidnapping, but you'd think—"

"It wasn't kidnapping," Devin protested. "And I won't go in front of a judge and jury and say that it was."

"Oh, sweetheart, he took you and kept you away from me, only allowing an occasional phone call. How can you say it wasn't kidnapping?"

"Just like I told Uncle Cam and all the police officers who asked me: I went with Uncle Mike willingly." Devin folded his spindly arms over his chest and scowled. "When he came upon me and that social worker who'd found me by the side of the road, do you think I didn't know who he was? That I couldn't have just told her who Uncle Mike was and kept him from taking me away?"

"I think perhaps you were trying to protect your Uncle Mike even then—and Julia, as well. You had no idea how desperate Michael's pursuit of the gold had become, or if he might hurt Julia."

Devin shook his head. "I never once thought he'd hurt her or me. I don't know why you're picking on Uncle Mike anyway. I mean, Uncle Cameron was the one who left me by the side of a highway with a pot of buried gold, and I don't see you blaming him for any of this."

Fiona winced.

"And that Julia Reed woman." Devin scowled. "Now that she and Uncle Cam are all lovey-dovey, I don't hear you saying anything bad about her and the way she just handed me over to Uncle Mike without even checking his ID or anything."

"He *was* dressed as a policeman," she reminded her son.

"He was dressed in a brown hat, pants, and shirt with a name tag and a badge that just had a number on it. It was his uniform from doing night security at an apartment complex." Devin's tone was matter-of-fact.

"He drove up to you and Julia with a red light flashin' from his dashboard—"

"And cops' lights are red and blue," Devin reminded her, as if that made Michael's actions perfectly legitimate.

"And he had a siren—"

"Actually, he just honked his horn. Miss Reed assumed she heard a siren. The traffic noise and thunder must have confused her—or maybe she just wanted to hear a police siren so she could be rid of me quickly. Of course, if I hadn't been left there on my own in the first place…"

Fiona gritted her teeth and looked away. They'd been through all this time and again. Still, she felt the need to defend her brother-in-law and the woman who had helped her get Devin home safely and put an end to this whole stolen-gold nonsense.

"When your Uncle Cam found the gold after all those years o' searchin', I'll admit he didn't use the best judgment leavin' you there alone with it. And Julia should have done more checkin' before handin' you over to *anyone*. But let's not lose sight of the fact that the real culprit—the one who held you hostage in return for gettin' his hands on the gold—was Michael Shaughnessy." She drew a deep breath, squared her shoulders, and tipped up her chin. "And I just wish he had been made to pay for his actions with more than a few weeks in jail while they sorted the whole thing through and decided not to prosecute the case for lack of evidence."

"He was doing what he thought was right, Mom, just like—" He cut himself off.

"Just like what, son?"

He shook his head. "Uncle Mike just did what he felt he had to do. To send him to jail for that would be as wrong as…as…as taking away the gold from my great-grandfather all those years ago."

Fiona groaned. "That's just a legend, Devin, my child—"

"I'm not a child," he grumbled, closing his textbook with a slam. "And if you'd just accept that, then maybe you could accept that I know my own mind, that I didn't testify against Uncle Mike for my own reasons—which are just as good as any grown-up's!"

He stood, tucked the book under his arm, and stormed off to his bedroom, leaving Fiona alone in the small apartment's living room.

She sighed, but that did not relieve the deep aching in her chest. She supposed she should be grateful that Devin had spoken to her at all about the event and his Uncle Mike—and more grateful still that however unsatisfactory the outcome, the ordeal of the gold, the family honor, and Michael Shaughnessy was forever over in their lives.

T w o

"Uniform. Hat. Keys." Michael tossed the items down on his former employer's desk. The overloaded key chain landed with a loud clunk.

"And the badge." The manager scrubbed his bulbous fingertips over his white-bristled jaw.

Michael dipped into his shirt pocket to retrieve the gleaming silver shield. It fell with a muted thud onto the pile.

"There," he said, turning on his heel. That done, he wanted out without further comment.

"I can't tell you how sorry I am to have to do this to you, Shaughnessy."

Benny's kind words, even spoken in his customary gruff tone, forced Michael to stop in his tracks.

"You were one of my best security guards," Benny went on. "Hard working, dependable, the residents liked you—"

"Liked. Past tense," Michael echoed. "Now they can't be rid of me fast enough. Management even moved me out of my apartment while I was in jail. Just packed up my things and changed the locks, no fuss, no muss. Had to spend last night in a motel across the river."

Benny grumbled a word that Michael couldn't quite make out, but he got the drift of it in the man's tone and narrowed eyes.

Michael shook his head, but he had to smile at Benny's peculiarly protective attitude. "I can't blame them for wanting to be rid of me, under the circumstances."

"Why?" The office chair groaned under the weight of Benny's barrel-chested build. "Police dropped them charges, didn't they?"

"Because they couldn't make a case, my friend, not because of my undeniable innocence." A ripple of guilt worked its way through him. He jerked his shoulder as though fighting back a twinge of pain. "If I still lived in these apartments, I sure wouldn't sleep well thinking the security of my home and family lay in the tainted hands of a man like me, a—what's the term?—a lowlife."

"Don't go talking like that," Benny grumbled.

"No use in sugarcoatin' it." Michael waved off any sympathy. "I was wrong. What I did was wrong. I took advantage of people's trust in me by letting them think I was a police officer."

A hard laugh sputtered from Benny's thick lips. "Ain't the first kid to do that. Probably won't be the last."

"But I'm no kid, Benny. I certainly knew better than to do it," Michael argued. "And that wasn't the worst of it."

He could almost hear Fiona's panicked voice as she begged him to let Devin come home. He'd known he was hurting her then, but he found a way to justify it. He did it for Devin, he convinced himself, for Neal and for all the O'Deas and Shaughnessys denied their rights. After all, he told himself, he'd planned to take the boy away for a time during spring break and again in the summer. He took excellent care of Devin as his mother had trusted him to do on those vacations, so it really wasn't so different than the trips he had planned.

And when his conscience—when something even deeper than human conscience—told him it *was* different, Michael had pushed it away. He had paid a great price for doing that— and so had Devin and Fiona. Every day, he wished for a way to make it up to them.

Michael swallowed hard, his eyes cast to the floor. "The worst of it is that I also hurt a lot of people that I really care for."

The other man snorted. "If we started firing people for that, we'd have to sign on a new staff every Monday morning."

Michael gave an obligatory chuckle and rubbed his fingers against the side of his neck, which freed the golden cross from inside his shirt collar.

Benny eyed the piece, his face lined with concentration. Michael half expected the man to mutter, "Oh, you're one of *those.*"

When he said nothing, Michael slid the cross back inside his shirt and nodded. "Thanks for all you've done for me, Benny."

"Wish it could be more." He leaned forward to place one forearm on the desktop. "How you fixed for money? You need a loan? Something to tide you over?"

"Actually, money I've got. Enough to see me through for a bit, anyway." He didn't bother to explain how he'd hoarded every cent he could for the last decade to fund his foolhardy treasure hunt. "What I need now is a place to rest my head at night and good honest work to occupy my hands by day."

Benny laughed. "You sure got a way of sayin' things. Maybe you could put that to use to get you what you need."

Michael thought of Fiona and Devin. The only thing he truly needed now had to come from them. "Blarney," he whispered.

"Huh?"

"That's what it's called, my friend. The gift of blarney. The ability to talk about anything and make it seem grander than it really is. And, in case you haven't been listening, 'tis that very gift that got me into this mess. If I'd been a wee bit less convincing, I might not have gotten so far in chasing my obsession."

"That there gold."

"Yes."

"Read all about it in the paper."

"You and every other person in the tristate area." Michael laughed, though he didn't find it amusing. "Going to make it plenty difficult to find a decent job until the news stories are long forgotten."

"Well, now, you see, that's where you use that gift of blarney. Use that, and me as a reference; maybe you'll do all right."

"Thanks, Benny."

"Don't mention it. Hope it all works out for you and you get whatever it is you need."

"What I need can't be worked for, Benny; it will have to be given, and I don't hold out too much hope that that will happen anytime soon, gift of blarney or no."

"I wouldn't be so sure of that." Benny swiveled in the chair, making it squawk in protest. He jabbed one finger toward the spot where Michael's cross had laid a moment ago. "God don't give us gifts lest he intends for us to use 'em. Trick is findin' a way to use 'em like the man upstairs would have you do it. You do that and I reckon you'll get what you need all right—and then some."

Michael started to contradict Benny but didn't get the chance.

"I know you, son. You got more going on for you than some might think. You know right from wrong, even if you don't always act on it, and you feel sorry for your mistakes. Kinda get the feeling you'd like to make up for them, too."

"If I only knew how—"

"You know how." Benny rolled his eyes heavenward. "Use the gifts God's given you and you'll find your way. Don't it say in the Bible somewheres that if you go looking for something you'll find it and if you knock on the door it's gonna open?"

"Somethin' like that."

"Well, then I reckon you better get to looking and knocking, Michael. God'll do the rest."

Michael didn't know whether Benny's wisdom or his comments about God surprised him more. Not that it mattered, as both gave him plenty to mull over as he tried to decide how to begin again—and how that new beginning might involve Fiona and Devin.

Fiona pressed her key into the lock of the shop's glass door. Placing her shoulder to the gilded words, Gadabout Gifts, she gave a stubborn shove and stumbled inside the cluttered store she'd been the manager of for the past two years.

She went about her morning routine without much thought to her actions: starting the coffeemaker, checking the cash drawer, giving the peculiar little shop full of antiques, collectibles, and imports the once-over for anything amiss. She didn't bother to relock the door, even though they did not officially open until ten o'clock. On a Monday morning in late May, she doubted if she would see a single customer until almost noon. She liked peaceful Mondays, liked the quiet time alone to organize her thoughts and plan for the week ahead.

The often absent owner had given her full charge of running the unique shop in the older but still trendy Mount Adams section of Cincinnati. She was his only employee, though they desperately needed another—someone to give her time off if she needed it or to fill in when she had dental appointments and whatnot. And it wouldn't hurt if that person had a strong back and a disposition for hard work.

The back room needed a thorough reorganization, and

there were heavy pieces of furniture around the shop that should have been moved and cleaned months ago. But the ads for help had gone unanswered, and Mr. Gadberry, the shop owner, hadn't really been concerned. He had Fiona, and he seemed quite content to work her into the ground without batting an eye or compensating her for her loyalty or her overtime.

She sighed. She didn't mind it that much, really, she told herself. And she had her motives for staying on. Fiona swiped a dark brown feather duster over a collection of mint-condition fashion dolls from the early seventies, but her gaze fell on the large case of imported Irish glassware. While the shop owner trusted her to take care of everything from the books to the inventory to the day-to-day dealings, he took on the much more fun and interesting job of buying the goods they carried. Someday, she hoped, all her devotion to her work would pay off and she'd be allowed to become a buyer as well.

She had good ideas, a real feel for what would sell, and a knack for selling it. The "gift of gab," her long-departed father would have called it. She moved around the shop whisking the duster here and there over clusters of knickknacks. In her heart she held a secret hope—a hope that, given the chance, she could help out her small village back in Ireland by bringing some of the local craftsmen's goods to America.

Her thoughts drifted back, as they often did, to the place she'd left not so long ago. Images from her homeland warmed her heart: the stone walls stretching across lush green hills, simple houses with smiling, ruddy-cheeked people in the doorways, always ready with a kind word. Quaint. That's how the folks of this city might describe the surroundings of her country. Provincial. That's what her husband had called it when he'd asked her to emigrate with him to America.

Fiona smiled to herself. Provincial or not, she saw it as a place with great potential. Of course, her view was not colored, as her husband's had been, by the constant comparisons, the gossip, the speculation, and the eerie adulation of some over the misdeeds of his grandfather. To spare her son the burden of growing up under the weight of the stolen gold and all the legends that surrounded it, she had agreed to move. She'd seen firsthand how that burden could cripple even a good man. Her father-in-law had been so affected. As had Michael.

There were no secrets in her hometown, least of all about the O'Deas and the Shaughnessys. Everyone knew that Michael Shaughnessy had had a brutal upbringing. His father, often too lost in the depths of drink or depression to care for the boy, clung to the tales of the stolen gold and how recovering it would redeem his family name and save them from their miserable existence.

After Michael's mother died, he was left to his own devices. The O'Dea family, the only ones in town who could truly appreciate the boy's situation, took him in. Or at least they tried, but it was a bit like trying to hold a thoroughbred to a trot, Fiona's father-in-law used to say. They took the boy to church, which seemed to tame that rogue spirit—for a time. But Michael was a breed born to run, a wild heart, with a mischievous glint in his eye and something that drove him always farther, faster, away from the ideas of home and family. She had learned that with painful clarity. Even all these years later, a subtle ache remained from the day the man she thought she would love her whole life had rejected her in favor of a stash of unseen coins.

Fiona's brother-in-law, Cameron, said he understood Michael's obsession with the gold because he shared it. Cameron wanted to find the gold to return it, to close the book on an ugly chapter in the family history so that he and all the O'Deas could move on. But Michael wanted something else entirely.

Fiona shivered and shook her head to free her mind of the dark memories and hurtful emotions that Michael conjured up. That was all behind her now. Cameron had taken the gold back to Ireland. Michael had been released from the charges of kidnapping, largely because of her son's refusal to testify. It was over. She'd never hear of that ruinous gold or see the roguish eyes of Michael Shaughnessy again.

She tucked the feather duster away and moved to the coffeepot. The dark, rich liquid made an almost melodic sound as she poured it into her favorite delicate china cup. Inhaling the steamy aroma, she wet her lips, peeked around the room, then dipped her fingers into a crystal bowl on the counter.

Plop. Plip. She dropped two small butterscotch candies into the brew and sighed at her little indulgence. Being a single mother, she had so few. Butterscotch was definitely her weakness. A sip of the sweet drink lifted her spirits and she strolled, cup in hand, past the door to the big picture window that looked out onto the sunlit side street.

"This is the day that the Lord has made," she whispered, raising her cup in salute to the picturesque scene. "Rejoice and be glad in it."

She took a long sip of coffee and wondered what Devin was doing in school right now and if she should, as his teacher urged, consider summer school to help him stay abreast of the other students. Summer school or no, she'd have to make some kind of plan in the next few weeks for the change in schedule when the regular school term let out. If only she weren't tied to this shop from nine to five.

She glanced at the tattered "Help Wanted" sign propped up

in the corner of the window and frowned. If she could find an assistant, her work hours would be much more flexible.

She watched a sparrow hop along a crumpled bit of side-walk, then spring up to a nest on the ledge atop the window. This spring, the partially hidden nook had made the perfect shelter for eggs and then tiny hatchlings. The sight made her think of how she needed to build a safe haven for her son. She wondered what the future held.

"Hello, Fiona."

The deep male voice resonated through her body, causing the cup to tremble in her hands.

Too late to be of any warning, the shop's front door fell shut with a noisy *whoosh*.

Her back stiff as wood, Fiona turned. "Michael Shaughnessy. What are you doing here? What is it you want?"

'Twas a good question, Michael thought. One he'd posed to himself as he passed the small shop time and again these past few days. Why *was* he here? And what did he want from Fiona O'Dea?

Absolution. Barring that—he met her gaze, her eyes made more vivid green by the paleness of her face—he would settle for a chance to explain. But for that to happen, he'd need time to show her that he had not changed so very much, time to help her trust him again, to enable her to listen to him.

He instantly saw in her eyes that the last thing she wanted was to listen, to give him the time he needed. His heart hammered in his ears at the realization of how deep her anger ran. His throat closed up. He'd been all wrong to come here. If he had any decency left in him, he'd turn and go, to leave this for another day.

"Fiona, I—" He glanced down at the dingy floor, the cluttered countertops, the crystal-clear front window.

A tiny brown bird with a twig in its beak fluttered from the ground to the top of the window. Michael blinked at the sight, thinking how gracious God was to care for the sparrows, and he knew that, though he certainly did not deserve it, God would provide for him as well.

His mind went to the verse Benny had tried to quote: *Seek and you will find.*

Then his eyes landed on the "Help Wanted" sign he'd never noticed before.

Ask and it will be given to you.

His lips tugged into a smile. "I came to apply for a job."

Three

A what?" She blinked her eyes in stark disbelief. "A job." He leaned forward to snatch up the dog-eared sign. "I believe you have an opening?"

"I believe you have an opening as well, Michael Shaughnessy—an opening in your head, and what little good sense you had seems to have slipped out of it." Anger started to seep through the numbing shock of his sudden appearance.

"Now, Fiona, let me—"

"No, Michael, *you* let *me*. Let me show you the way to the door." She flung her arm out to direct the way. "And while I'm about it, let me assure you that there is no way on this green earth I'd let you work for me!"

He cocked his head. His feet didn't budge. "Why not? I need a job. You have a job that needs filling. Is that such a stretch of the imagination?"

"Yes, I think it is, given the situation, Michael." She reached out to yank the sign from his hand. "I'll thank you now to be taking your leave."

"So you're saying the job is filled, then?"

She took a step back. "I'm saying there is no job—not for you. Now will you be going or shall I call the police?"

"The police? Are you really *that* afraid, Fiona?"

She searched the clash of emotions running riot within her, but fear was not among them. She searched his eyes. Though they were older, with fine lines fanning out from the corners, they were the same eyes of the man she'd called sweetheart and friend. Despite everything, she could not fear this man.

Michael held his arms open wide. "It's just me, after all—the smudged-faced boy who grew up in the streets outside your doorstep, who stood behind you and tweaked your pigtails in the church choir of an Easter morning, who—"

"You've changed, Michael; you cannot deny that."

"So have you, Fiona." His eyes fixed on hers. "More than my misdeeds and the pain of the past months have changed you. I know that better than anyone."

"Don't, Michael...."

"I was never an angel, Fiona, not like Cameron. Not like Neal."

The mention of her late husband made her shoulders tense. "Neal was no angel, nor is Cameron."

"But neither of them struggled as I have to find their way, Fiona. You know that."

She conceded with a nod.

"And still, lost as I was, uncertain, always sure to make a mistake, you never held it against me." He reached out to lift her chin with his bent knuckle. "I realized that sitting in the jail. You always found it in your heart to forgive me, Fiona, when no other human could."

"Don't ask me to forgive you this time, Michael. Not yet. My heart tells me I should; my faith tells me I must. But I'm not ready."

"Then don't forgive me yet, Fiona. But don't turn me out, either."

The naked plea in his voice touched her heart. Still, she rallied her defenses. "Isn't there someplace else you could find work?"

"Who would have me, darlin' girl?"

The use of the old endearment made her wince. The pads

of her fingertips flattened to the sign pressed over her thudding heart.

"My foolish shenanigans and contemptible face have made the news time and again these weeks past. No one who saw that would give me a chance." He placed his hands on his lean hips. "If you don't hire me, I've nowhere else to go."

"I think you're overstating things a bit." She relaxed and rolled her eyes.

"What's the matter, Fiona? Are you afraid I'll steal from you?"

"No, of course not."

"That I'll drive away the customers?"

She stole a peek at him. Truth to tell, that handsome face and hint of brogue would enchant more than one of her regular lady customers and perhaps bring in new ones to boot. "No, that's not it."

"Then you really don't have need of another worker? It's something that can wait awhile?"

Devin's schedule change, her own weariness, and the opportunity to become more than a workaday lackey to her boss all required that she hire someone soon. Yesterday, if possible. "No, I need to hire someone."

"Just not me."

She looked away.

"Well, then." He slapped his hands against his thighs. "I guess that's it. If you won't hire me, I don't hold out much hope that anyone will—not for a while, at least."

She hated to see him discouraged so, but what could she do? *Hire him,* something in her mind whispered, while every other fiber in her being rebelled.

"Sorry to trouble you, Fiona."

"I only wish you'd thought that way before you made off with Devin."

She saw the regret flash through his eyes.

He dipped his head in good-bye to her, then turned. He walked away slowly, like a man carrying a great burden. The May morning sunlight streamed in over his broad shoulders and caught the red color in his hair. For one fleeting instant, he was that young man in Ireland who had walked out of her life fifteen years ago. A man whose heart and mind seemed always in conflict, unsettled, in need of just a trace more compassion than she had to give.

Hire him. She looked around the shop at all the loathsome work piling up, thought of the time she wanted to take off this summer for Devin, and of the future she could build for her child if she could advance in her job. Michael could give her the time she needed and an honest day's work, which seemed a rarity these days.

She drew in a long breath, held it, then released it with one long rush. She'd probably regret what she was about to do for a very long time. "The owner would have to give final approval."

"What's that?" He turned his head to eye her over his shoulder.

"The owner of the shop. He retains final say over all hiring." She whacked the "Help Wanted" sign down onto the counter and strode forward. "Of course, he trusts my judgment implicitly."

"Wise man."

"We'll see about that," she murmured. She reached for the handle and pulled the heavy door open. "You can start tomorrow, ten o'clock sharp."

"I can't believe you're going for this, Fiona."

"Why not? As you pointed out, you need a job, and I need an employee. No one else would have the strength to put up with you but me—how can I argue with that logic?"

"How indeed?" A smile lit his face from his strong jaw to his sparkling eyes.

"Tomorrow," she said, pushing him out the door, then tugging it shut between them. As she watched him stroll off, hands in his jeans pockets, whistling a jaunty tune, she couldn't help but smile herself. "We'll see if you're still whistling this time tomorrow when you discover just what it is you've gotten yourself into, Michael Shaughnessy."

A bead of sweat trickled down Michael's neck and into his T-shirt. "What have you gotten yourself into, Michael, me boy?" he muttered in a lilt reminiscent of his childhood.

"And when you're through moving that armoire, you can—"

"Take a break?" he suggested, dragging the back of his hand over his forehead.

"Mop the floor," Fiona finished. She shifted her weight from one foot to the other as she stood behind the glass counter where the cash register stood.

Prim as you please, she had a pencil tucked behind one ear, and her white blouse and pale skirt were fresh as when she had arrived this morning. Rifling through a confusion of papers before her, she showed no interest in Michael's hard work or his welfare.

He placed one shoulder to the armoire and pushed. The screeching complaint of wood scooting over tile rang in his ears. That should get her attention, he thought.

"Be careful," she said, thumbing through pages.

"How's that?" He stood back and wiped his hands down his jeans, determined that she would notice his effort.

"A little more to the left. You'll need to be able to mop behind it." She raised her coffee cup, then set it down again without drinking. "And once the mopping is done, you can—"

"Take a break." It was no suggestion this time. He'd been hard at it since ten o'clock this morning, and the wall clock read half past one already.

Fiona crinkled up her nose. "Yes, I suppose you can take a break then—while the floor dries."

"Thank you ever so much," he groaned, as he gave the lumbering piece of furniture one last shove. He straightened. "Done."

"You'll find the mop in the back of the storeroom near the sink, with the bucket just beneath." She didn't even look up from her papers.

Terrific. He'd finagled his way into this job for the sole purpose of spending time with Fiona, and she hardly noticed his presence. Well, he'd see what he could do about that.

"Fiona, darlin', after the mopping is done, how about some lunch?"

"Hmm?" She glanced up but not at him directly, then fumbled through her papers and plucked up a red pen. "I told you to take your break. Whether you use it to eat lunch or take up knitting is up to you."

"No, I meant you and I should have lunch."

The papers rustled as she shifted them about. "I can't leave the shop."

"But I could bring something in—for the both of us."

Her hand stilled. Her tongue tipped out to dab at the corner of her mouth.

"I noticed a sandwich shop around the way. Maybe a bit of roast beef on wheat bread with some of those wavy potato chips you so favor on the side...." If he'd waved the plate right under her nose, he couldn't have asked for a better response.

She shut her eyes and inhaled as if she could smell the food even now.

"What do you say, Fiona? It would only take me a minute to run and fetch it, then you and I could—"

Her eyes came open; her jaw set. "The only thing you and I are going to do is this: You are going to mop the floor, then take your break. I am going to finish going over these invoices."

"But you have to eat."

"I brought my lunch from home, thank you."

"We could still eat at the same time."

"No, we can't. Somebody has to man the front of the store while the other eats in back."

He folded his arms over his chest. "Don't tell me that when you worked here alone you ate your lunch in the back."

"No, I didn't. But now that you're here, I have that luxury." She shuffled the invoices into one stack and tapped the edges on the countertop to align them. "Now, don't you have a date with a mop?"

"Lucky me. I suppose by this afternoon you'll have me engaged—in cleaning the storeroom, no doubt," he muttered as he moved through the doorway.

"No. Actually, we'll take turns working in the storeroom next week." She picked up her fragile-looking cup filled with the coffee she'd been nursing all morning and topped it off. "That way you can get some front-room experience with me nearby to help out."

"Good." He stepped across the threshold into the storeroom, then craned his neck to watch her move about the shop. She balanced her cup on the matching saucer, glanced at the front door, then, quick as a child sure to be caught, snatched some butterscotch candy from a dish and dropped it into her drink.

He'd forgotten how much she loved butterscotch and how guilty she felt about indulging in it. He'd forgotten so many things about the girl he'd once asked to share his life. Her straightforwardness, her simple beauty, her inner strength.

How he would love spending these next few weeks, or however long it took him to regain her trust and forgiveness, learning about Fiona all over again.

"It isn't so bad, working with me, is it, Fiona?" he asked softly.

"No, not too bad." She turned to look at him and made a face as though it were marginally tolerable.

"Something you could get used to, right?" he urged, wanting some sign that she could in any way warm to him.

"If I had to, I suppose I could learn to deal with it, but since I don't have to—"

He straightened, the movement making his damp shirt cling to his back like a clammy rag. "What do you mean? We are going to work together, aren't we?"

"We will next week some, but once you've learned the ropes, our schedules will be opposites."

"Opposites?"

"Yes, you'll work the days and hours that I take off, and vice versa. Why else is it you think I hired you, Michael?"

He gripped the door frame until the old wood bit into his palm and managed to give her a casual shrug. "Because you needed me and—because we needed each other?"

"I need you all right. I need you to be here when I can't." She took a long sip of her coffee, then settled both saucer and cup onto the counter with a *clink*. She raised her eyes to his, smoothed one hand down her pristine skirt, and said, "If everything goes according to plan, we'll hardly ever see each other again."

~ ~ ~ ~ ~

Fiona yanked at the waistband of her grubbiest jeans and stuffed the shirttail of her raggedy Kings Island T-shirt firmly in place. Adjusting the scarf that covered most of her hair but for a few wayward curls, she drew in a deep breath and turned to confront her nemesis.

A low groan came from between her clenched teeth. "Why did I put off cleaning out this storeroom for so long?"

"Because you were waiting for a leprechaun to creep in at night and do it for you?" She turned to see Michael in the doorway.

She gave his gray dress slacks, the subtle pattern on his vest, and his banded-collar shirt the once-over. "Don't you look nice?"

"'Tis my first day out front without my meddlesome boss hovering over my every move. Thought I'd try to make a good impression."

On whom? she thought. She didn't ask it aloud because she didn't want to hear the answer. He'd impress the customers cloaked in nothing more than his native charm and a grungy sweatsuit. But if it was her he had in mind to impress...

She studied the thick waves of his dark hair, the quiet eyes framed by faint laugh lines, the hint of a smile on his lips. The last thing she wanted was to be any more impressed with this man.

No, she thought, she'd take that back. The last thing she wanted was to spend any more time with Michael than absolutely necessary.

"Well, as an old hand at working in the shop, let me give you this little hint that will make it so much easier for you."

"What's that, darlin' girl?"

"When working the front of the shop…"

"Yes?"

"It's best to be *in* the front of the shop." She poked one finger in that direction.

"As always, I bow to your superior experience." The man actually made a little bow, then turned on his heel and headed into the shop, humming.

Humming! She snarled. Easy for him to do. He wasn't facing the leaning tower of packing crates. She gulped air that carried the stench of mold and the dusty odor of the excelsior that was scattered over the floor and dangled from empty wooden boxes.

"What a mess," she mumbled, debating silently just where to begin to tackle it all.

Near the front of the dark, drafty back room, the desk caught her attention. Stacks of catalogs put aside for a day when she had time to go through them taunted her. Beside them lay files of paperwork that she should have entered into the new computer system last week. Maybe if she just took a moment to see to some of that…

From the front of the shop, the clinks and clatters of the morning routine drifted back to her as if Michael were saying, "I'm busy, why aren't you?"

No, she couldn't be sidetracked. The sooner the storeroom got sorted out, the sooner she could stop spending so much time with Michael.

She smiled, thinking of her son's reaction last week when she told him she'd hired Michael to work in the shop. Devin, putting on the self-assured face of the man of the family, told her she'd done the right thing. She only hoped that Cameron would feel the same when he returned from Ireland and found Michael here. Not that Cameron's approval or disapproval would change anything, but it would be nice to have his support.

She sighed and pivoted to face the real work, the dirty, muscle-straining, put-it-off-so-long-it-turned-into-a-monster work that she'd promised herself she would do. She grabbed a trash bag and wrestled with the thin plastic to peel apart the opening. That done, she set about gathering up the trash. Packing material, bits of wood, and copper staples flew into the bag as fast as her fingers could collect them. Still, she hardly seemed to make any progress. She'd be half the day doing this, and in the end she'd create enough garbage to fill the huge dumpster behind the shop. She scowled.

She needed a system. She made a quick sweep of the surroundings until her gaze landed on the empty crates perched precariously one on top of the other.

"That's it." She tossed the bag to one side and marched up to the crates, which loomed a good two feet over her head. "Let's see.... One crate for rubbish, one for packing material to keep on hand to use again, one for paper to take to the recycling bin."

Three crates should do nicely for starters, she decided. Stretching on tiptoe, she tried to work her fingers over the edge of the highest crate. The rough wood scraped at the skin of her arms. She couldn't quite reach. Maybe she should call Michael in to help.

From the front room the full-bodied aroma of fresh coffee wafted back. Michael's hum broke into a low, deep song she hadn't heard in years. The mingling of the two warmed her inside, and without further introspection, she began to hum along as she moved toward the door into the bright front of the shop.

"How may I help you this good day?" Michael coated the question with a thick helping of the old brogue.

Fiona shook her head when she realized that he had spoken to a customer and not to her. She blinked. What had she been about to do? Seek out Michael Shaughnessy—the man she was working to be rid of—for help?

"I think not," she mumbled under her breath. She could do this. After all, it was only a few crates. A bit of a reach. Nothing more.

She wiped her hands along her faded jeans, rotated her shoulders to better loosen herself up, then poked out her tongue to better her concentration and focus her effort. Up on her toes she went again, arms outstretched.

"Almost got it." Splinters jabbed through her T-shirt and gouged her skin. "Just a wee bit…"

Her fingertips curved over the top crate's rim.

The tower wobbled.

Fiona steadied it with one hand and gave a great jerk with the other.

"If there's anything I can be helping you with," came Michael's voice, "don't hesitate to—"

Crash!

"Yeeooooww!" Fiona howled as crates slammed into her cheek, neck, shoulder, and stomach on their way to the floor. She landed on her bottom in the middle of the wreckage.

"Holler," Michael finished when the last crate had cracked against the concrete. "Fiona, are you all right?"

"I'm fine," she called back.

"Are you sure? It sounded like—" His voice drew nearer.

"I'm fine," she insisted, struggling to leap to her feet despite the twinge in her side that told her to stay seated. He wouldn't catch her lying down on the job—or sprawling as the case may be. "I just had a little…mishap. Don't bother yourself about it. Some crates fell on the floor."

"Looks like some crates fell on *you*." He strode into the storeroom, stopping less than an arm's length away from her.

"They missed me." *Mostly,* she justified the fib to herself without meeting his eyes.

"Oh, then I suppose you were just wearing this for decoration?" He plucked a tangle of excelsior from the curl along her cheek.

"That stuff is everywhere back here. So what if a little got stuck to me while I went about my work?" She batted his hand away.

"I didn't mean that. I meant this." His hand came again to her face, and his fingers curved to gently stroke the scrape from her cheek to her chin.

She winced at the coolness of his touch over the sudden sting of her raw skin.

"You're hurt," he whispered.

"Nonsense." She angled her chin up but not away from his light caress. "Now go and tend to your customer."

He hesitated, the back of his hand lingering over her temple.

"Go on with you." She jerked her head toward the door.

He held her gaze a moment more, then sighed and let his hand drop away.

The absence of his touch made her pulse leap as if it had held still these last few seconds, then raced to catch up.

"I'll go, if you're sure you're all right," he said.

"Go!" She swung her arm out to reinforce the command.

Searing pain ripped through her side. She gasped as her legs went watery.

Michael caught her by the arm before her knees buckled completely. "See? You're not all right."

"I must have pulled a muscle." She sucked in a long breath between her lips.

"Are you sure that's all it is?"

She nodded.

"You don't think I should be calling a doctor?"

She shook her head.

He helped her to the nearest chair, and she settled into it with relief. The pain subsided to a dull throb.

"I just need to rest a minute to catch my breath," she said, making herself as comfortable as possible. "Then I'll be good as new. You go see to your customer."

He went down on one knee before her. "I'd rather see to you."

His hands found hers. His gaze fixed on her eyes. He said no more, but wet his lips as though he wished he could.

A girl with greater sense would have given him a stern warning just then and sent him back to work. But where Michael Shaughnessy was concerned, it seemed that Fiona had no sense at all.

"Thank you, Michael. I appreciate your kindness."

"Now, there are words I never thought I'd hear from you. Maybe I should check your head for bumps."

"Try it and you'll be getting your own bump for your trouble," she growled through a grin.

"That sounds more like my girl." He patted her hand, then stood. "You sit here, and I'll get you a cup of coffee."

"No, I—"

But he had already left.

Thank you, Michael. I appreciate your kindness. She mouthed the words with a mocking expression. What had gotten into her? Could those crates have hit her square on the head and made her forget what the man had done to her?

She pulled the scarf from her hair and used it to dab at the tiny thread of blood across her arm. As soon as Michael got back here, she would tell him a thing or two. First, that she'd hired him to work in the shop, not to play nursemaid. Second, that she could take care of things—her aches and pains as well as her responsibilities in the storeroom—very well on her own. And third, that the sooner they got the storeroom job finished and began their separate work schedules, the better.

They'd spent far too much time together already. That's what she'd tell him, and—

"Fiona?"

She looked up to find him standing over her, her special coffee cup and saucer dwarfed by his huge hand.

"Hmm?" Way to tell him off, she thought.

"Your coffee."

"Oh." She blinked at the dark liquid. She wasn't exactly in the mood for coffee, especially without her butterscotch mixed in. Still, that was no reason to be rude. She accepted the cup. "Thank you."

"Drink that and relax," he suggested.

She waited a moment for him to return to the shop, but he seemed content to stand there, hands in his pockets, watching her.

"I really don't have time for a coffee break now, Michael." She set the saucer in her lap and arched her eyebrows pointedly at him, adding, "And neither do you."

He chuckled, that deep, comfortable chuckle that resonated like a fond memory through her.

"The customer has gone, if that's what you're worried about. And I can see the front door from here, so if anyone else comes in…" He let his voice trail off and tilted his head. "Now, take a sip."

"Michael, I don't—"

"One sip," he urged.

He wasn't going to let this go. "All right, if that's what it takes to get you to go on about your business."

She lifted the cup to her lips. A familiar aroma filled her senses. Could it be? She took a swallow of the brew; it slid over her tongue and filled her mouth with her favorite flavor. Butterscotch.

"How did you know?"

He gave her a wink but no answer.

She smiled up at him in return.

"You finish that up and then—"

"And then I have to get back to work—and so do you."

"Work, fine, but no more of the lifting of crates and such for you." He wagged his finger at her.

"Oh?" She sputtered her lips together. "You know of some unemployed leprechauns who'll do it for me?"

"No, but I know of one oversized leprechaun who is already employed by this shop who will do it."

"You?"

"Me."

"You're hardly dressed for manual labor today." She savored another swallow of coffee.

"But I will be tonight when I come back after hours."

"I can't let you do that."

"Why not?"

"Well, because it's hardly fair. I said I'd do it—in fact, I need to do it, to organize things and so on. I can't allow you to take this on by yourself."

"Who said anything about my cleaning out this whole storeroom by myself?" He folded his arms and leaned his shoulders back. "You don't pay me enough for that, darlin' girl."

"I'm almost afraid to ask this, but what did you have in mind?"

"You supervise; I exercise. It's the perfect solution, and working together we can get most of it done tonight."

Fiona set the cup on its saucer. "I just don't think—"

"You mean you don't have any other work to do around here that needs your brain and not your brawn?" He gave her arm a squeeze. "Not that you don't have the muscle power for it, of course."

Fiona could not hide her smile at his gentle teasing. She also could not forget the stack of catalogs she practically itched to get into. "Well, there are a few things that need my attention."

"Good. It's settled then." From the front of the shop the sound of the door sweeping open made him perk up. "I've got to go back now. You rest. Do what you can around here—without lifting a finger. And come tonight, you and I will stay here as long as it takes to get the job done—together."

Four

Pizza delivery!" Michael raised the box high over his head as he wound his way through Gadabout Gifts toward the storeroom.

They'd closed up the shop at the usual time, then gone their separate ways, agreeing to meet back in the storeroom at six o'clock. It would have taken too long for him to go all the way back to the modest motel he called home these past weeks, so Fiona had offered to bring him some work clothes from her home while he picked up a pizza.

Michael could hardly contain his optimism about this evening as he came into the darkened storeroom. He flipped on the light and set down the box. Why Fiona thought the two of them would need an extra large with extra everything he could not imagine, but he didn't question her choice. He was spending the evening with her, and that was all that mattered.

He'd made a breakthrough with her today; he'd felt it in her reaction to his butterscotch-coffee surprise and in the very fact that she'd agreed to his plan that would ensure them more time together—alone.

"Michael? That *is* you back there, isn't it?" The front door fell shut over the sound of footsteps and Fiona's voice.

Michael swept his hand back through his hair, cleared his throat, and turned. "'Tis me for sure.... Devin?"

"Hi, Uncle Mike." The sober-faced boy thrust his hand out.

Michael glanced down at the formal gesture from the boy who had once come running into his arms. A lump formed in his throat. How he wished he could draw him into a tight hug, to tell him how sorry he was for all he'd done. But Devin wouldn't accept it any more than Fiona would. Michael had done too much damage, and the boy's stiff behavior drove that point painfully home.

Fiona came up behind her son, and Michael asked her with a glance if she'd permit the contact with Devin.

She gave him an encouraging nod.

The boy's thin hand disappeared inside Michael's grasp. He gave it a firm shake, saying, "I know it's small comfort for me to say it now, but I am sorry for what I did."

Devin's eyes darted to follow Fiona's movements. The boy kept his hand clasped to Michael's until she had passed them both and walked back to hang her purse on a coat hook. When she was out of hearing range, he leaned in close and whispered, "You don't have to apologize to me, Uncle Mike. I'm not mad at you."

"You're not?"

He shook his head.

"But I—"

"You did what you thought you had to do," he said, sounding far more mature than his age.

"I owe you my thanks for telling the cops I didn't kidnap you, even though—"

The boy shrugged and cut him off. "I did what *I* had to do."

The gravity of tone and expression almost brought a smile to Michael's lips, but he reined it in so as not to embarrass the boy. "Well, I thank you, just the same."

"We Shaughnessys and O'Deas, we have to stick together."

Before Michael could ask Devin just what it was he meant by that, Fiona came up to them.

"Well, did you get the pizza?"

He put his hand atop the box. "Either that or they've given me a cake that's been run over by a steamroller."

"I don't care which it is." She waved her hand. "I'm so hungry I could eat either—or both."

Her smile seemed pinched. Clearly, having them all together here put a real strain on her.

"Devin, me boy," he said, his gaze on Fiona even as he turned his head to speak to her son, "it seems I left the napkins and the bottle of soda out in my car. Could you go and get them for us?"

Devin hesitated, then he gave a nod. "Sure. Do you still have that plain white car?"

The reference to the nondescript car that had fooled more than one person into thinking it was an unmarked police vehicle made Michael flinch.

"Um, no, I have a red compact—it's parked right by the curb." He tossed his keys to the boy. "You can't miss it."

"I'll be right back." Devin raised the keys in salute as he backed out the door.

When they were alone, Michael reached out to brush his hand over Fiona's shoulder. "I'm glad you brought him tonight, Fiona. I know it can't have been an easy thing for you to do."

"Well, I couldn't leave him alone." She slipped away from his touch.

"Of course not."

"And…" She spun the pizza box around on the cluttered back-room table so that it would open facing her. "And the truth is, he wanted to come. He wanted to see you."

"Still, it took a lot of faith for you to allow it."

"Faith?"

"In your son. And in the Lord. I'm sure you prayed about whether or not to expose your child to the man who carried him off and kept him away from you."

"You're more than that, Michael, and you know it," she said softly. "When Neal died, you were so helpful to us. And you did so many things with Devin, helped him at school, took him fishing. You were like a—"

Father. She didn't say it, and she didn't need to. Few people knew as he did how hard Neal had been on Devin, how distant their relationship had been. Michael supposed he'd overindulged the boy in those months after Neal's death, but he'd enjoyed it. And some part of him had always thought of Devin as the closest thing he'd ever have to his own child.

"I did pray before I came here tonight, Michael, but not about whether I should let Devin see you again." Fiona ran her fingers along the edge of the white box.

"What did you pray for, Fiona?"

"You." She lifted her gaze to his.

"Me?"

"I prayed you'd find your way again."

"I think I have, darlin' girl." He unfastened the top button of his shirt, then raked his fingers back through his hair. The golden cross that he'd designed slid free to gleam in the dim overhead light.

Fiona's attention fell to the piece. She smiled a sad smile, then looked away. "I hope you have, Michael. For your sake as well as Devin's."

What about your own sake? He wanted to ask, but the tightness in his throat strangled back his voice.

"It seems like you have changed, Michael," she went on. "Without the plague of that wretched gold, it seems these last few days you've been more and more like that dear boy I once…"

He reached his hand out to stroke her cheek.

She tossed her hair—or did she turn into his caress?

The shop door swished open and shut, and Devin's rubber-soled shoes squeaked across the floor.

Fiona stepped back, finishing the thought. "You are more and more like the boy I once knew."

He wanted to ask if that meant she had forgiven him, or that perhaps she *could* forgive him once he'd convinced her the changes were not contrived or phantoms of her own wishful thinking. But Devin burst on the scene just then, his arms full and his stomach apparently empty.

"Food! Give me food!" he bellowed in a false bass voice.

"Here, give me those." Fiona pulled the soda bottle and the flapping napkins from the boy's arms. "Now, pour yourself one of these while I dish up the pizza."

The moment had passed, and the only thing left for Michael to do was hope for another opportunity alone with Fiona. Given that after tonight they would work on differing schedules, he could only guess when that might be.

"Is there any of that pizza left?"

"Pizza?" Fiona rolled her eyes and shook her head at her son. "It's well onto midnight, Devin. How can you think of eating cold leftover pizza now?"

"I'm hungry," he protested.

"You're always hungry," she countered.

"Especially when my mother works me half to death moving boxes and hauling trash."

"Michael did twice the work that you did, and you don't see him—"

"Hmm?" Michael, who'd been standing with his back to them, turned, a slice of pizza halfway to his lips.

"Oh, for pity's sake. You two!" She pretended to scowl at the pair, but a cozy warmth seeped through her.

Devin accepted the last slice of pizza from Michael and grinned broadly at her as they both gobbled down their late-night snack.

She hadn't seen Devin grin since...since the last time he'd been around his Uncle Mike. The old Michael who loved and protected him, that is, not the one who'd used him to further a hopeless cause. That sober reminder cooled the glow of the moment. Fiona nabbed her purse from the hook on the wall.

"It's late, son; we'd best hurry on home." She slung the strap over her shoulder. "I thank you, Michael, for your help."

"It does look much better, doesn't it?" He set the remnant of his slice aside and folded his arms over the plain blue sweat-shirt of Cameron's she'd brought for him to work in.

"Yes. I never realized how much room we have back here."

"And you accomplished a fair bit of work yourself, didn't you?"

If she didn't know better, she'd suspect him of stalling to keep her from leaving quite so soon.

"Well, I filed everything and did my computer work, then went through all the catalogs and put little sticky notes on the pages of things I hope Mr. Gadberry will order." She sighed. "Not that it will do much good."

"Why not?" Michael leaned against the wall, as though preparing for a lengthy conversation.

"I haven't the time or the strength to go into it all now, Michael, but suffice it to say the only thing that man listens to is his own inflated opinion of his supposed good taste." She folded her arms in a tight hug over her chest. "He thinks only he knows best what to stock and try to sell, even though he's never spent an hour working in the store since I've been here.

He just pops in to check up on me now and again. Oh, and to clutter the back desk with invoices for me to file for things I'll have to dust for the next six months before I mark them down to get rid of them."

"Sounds charming."

"Oh, he's not a bad fellow; it's just that—"

"It's just that you work hard for him, and the very least he could do is give your input some consideration."

"Why, yes." The tightness of her folded arms loosened.

"You wish he trusted you more."

"Exactly." She blinked up at Michael.

"Of course, how can he learn to trust you if he won't take the time to find out if you're worthy of that trust?"

"Why do I have the feeling we're not talking about Mr. Gadberry anymore?" She narrowed her eyes in suspicion.

"Do you have that feeling, Fiona?" He smiled, his eyes wide with innocence. "And who is it you think we'd be talking about then, if not the man himself?"

"You know good and well who." If her eyes had been any more fiery, Michael would have had a hole burned straight through him at that moment.

Enigmatic. Fiona hardly ever had cause to use such a word, but Michael's grin—part rogue, part saint, all charm—called for it.

Without admitting a thing, he graciously sidestepped the issue as he nodded to her and said, "Well, to hear you speak of him, I am looking forward to meeting this Mr. Gadberry."

"And he's looking forward to meeting you."

"At least he trusted your judgment enough to give you approval over the phone to hire me," Michael reminded her.

"We'll see how long that approval lasts. He'll be back from his buying trip on Monday." She watched Devin gnaw down to the crust on his slice of pizza. "So I suppose you won't see him unless he makes a point of coming in while you're working."

"Or if I come in when he's here." He eyed her with thinly veiled interest.

"I'd rather you didn't. I'll have enough to handle with just him." She shook her head. "Heaven alone knows what bit of repulsive bric-a-brac he'll be carting in, expecting me to know just what to do with the thing."

Michael opened his mouth, and she expected an argument from him, but Devin's voice intervened instead.

"I'm finished with my pizza, Mom."

She hitched her purse strap high on her shoulder and gave Michael a little wave. "Well, that's it, then. We need to hurry on home."

Michael shut his mouth; then he sighed.

"All right, then, I'll get the lights." He strode to the small bank of switches that operated the lights in the storeroom and in the shop. "Devin, do you still have the keys to the back door from when you took the trash to the dumpster?"

"They're in my—" he tried to reach around the pizza box in his arms—"back pocket."

"Never mind the keys," Michael said. "You can give them to your mom later. Just bring the box to throw away when we get outside."

"What, no instructions for me?" Fiona opened her hands to tease him for his sudden take-charge attitude.

"You, darlin' girl," he said, pointing his finger, "have the most important job of all. You'll have to lead the way in the dark through this maze of a shop of yours."

"Yes, sir." She gave a sharp salute.

There, she'd done it, Fiona thought as she waited for the fellows to take care of the last details; she'd survived the whole evening with Michael. From now on the closest she'd ever have to come to the man were on the days she'd hand him his work schedule or paycheck across the counter. She stepped into the darkness of the musty smelling shop.

"I could navigate this shop with my eyes closed," she boasted. "One false step could knock over something very expensive, so stick close to me."

"I'll be fine, Mom," Devin called.

"Well, I'm still learning the lay of the land as it were." Michael placed his hand on her waist and moved so near she could feel his breath stir the curls over her ear as he whispered, "I'm with you, Fiona. Right behind you every step of the way."

He felt her shudder. No, more the suggestion of a shudder. And it made him smile. Slowly, with patience and kindness, he'd win her acceptance of him as a friend, and from that, hopefully her forgiveness.

That he didn't seem to need to earn Devin's forgiveness relieved him in some ways and disturbed him in others. What on earth had the boy meant earlier when he said they'd both done what they had to do and that the Shaughnessys and O'Deas had to stick together? Had his influence over Devin so instilled the old legend, the old anger that burned so hot it consumed what was good until only the obsession remained?

He glanced over his shoulder, his eyes adjusting to the darkness, to check on the boy following behind them.

Along with making himself a part of Fiona's life again, he knew he must make inroads into his relationship with Devin as well. The boy needed gentle discipline, an unwavering male role model such as Michael himself had never known. He also needed to know that even role models fall short of the mark from time to time and have to be forgiven.

"Watch out for this table, now; it's a jog to the left and a bit of a tight squeeze," Fiona said, shifting sideways to navigate the passage between the counter and a display table.

Michael did as she said, but his leg bumped the corner of the table, and he sucked in his breath at the stab of pain.

"Are you all right?" Her tone, infused with genuine concern, eased the discomfort considerably.

"I'm fine." He reached out to her again. "I guess I just wasn't following closely enough."

"You were doing just fine at that distance," she assured him.

Michael chuckled. Her light reprimand sounded more like amused agitation. That was a vast improvement, he decided, from the coldness and even hostility of the past. He'd made headway. Given time and closeness, he'd make more, he felt sure.

"This just isn't as easy as I expected," Fiona went on. "Since we close at five, I'm rarely in here after dark."

Devin rammed into the same corner that had gouged Michael, letting out an *ooph* in the dark. Something on the table wobbled, then toppled, but it did not sound as though it broke.

"I wish I had thought to bring a flashlight," Michael grumbled.

Fiona came to a dead stop.

Michael collided with her.

Devin came up just short of bumping into Michael.

Fiona whirled around.

Michael found her almost in his arms, her face upturned so that what little light there was shone in her eyes and over her parted lips. A gentleman might have stepped back then. He didn't. "What is it, Fiona?"

She met his gaze. "I…um…there's a flashlight in the storeroom, just inside the door."

Michael put his hands on her arms, his eyes on hers.

"Maybe we should send Devin back to get—"

"You're not sending anybody anywhere." A bright beam of light targeted them from near the front door. "Stay right where you are and put your hands in the air."

Even as they obeyed the gruff voice beyond the blinding light, Michael said, "Look, if you're here to rob the place, you have our full cooperation; just don't harm the boy or—"

"Fiona, is that you?"

She spun around, one of her raised hands moving to shadow her eyes. "Mr. Gadberry? Is that *you*?"

"Yes, I—"

Feet scuffed, the light wiggled, and two men's voices mumbled out unfinished phrases as they obviously fumbled for control of the high-powered flashlight. Finally, one man triumphed, and he raised it like the torch of freedom for a moment before aiming it under the fleshy rolls of his own chin.

"It *is* you," Fiona cried.

"Yes, it is, and I—"

"Is everything all clear, sir?" the second man asked, his tone doubtful.

"Of course it's all clear. Would I be carrying on a conversation with burglars?" Gadberry harrumphed. "Someone save me from these private security setups—"

He gestured with the light, sending the bright shaft spinning across the face of a man in uniform and then around the shop.

"I wonder if they're worth the money I pay them to—" Gadberry clucked his tongue and interrupted himself to address the man beside him. "Well, would you make yourself useful and go turn on a light?"

"Um, I have to radio back to the office and tell them it's a false alarm, Mr. Gadberry." The second man retrieved the flashlight, which revealed his khaki uniform and whipcord lean frame.

"I'll turn on the lights," Devin volunteered.

"What? Who was that?"

"My son, Devin, is here," Fiona answered. "And Michael, the new man I hired."

"We've been cleaning out the storeroom, Mr. Gadberry," Michael said.

"Storeroom?"

"Yes, the back of the shop," Fiona clarified.

"Oh, the back of the shop," Gadberry echoed. "Yes, good job. I thought maybe—"

The overhead lights hummed, then sputtered, and finally flicked on to shine in an eerie glow around them.

Michael automatically closed his eyes at the sudden light, then opened them to find Gadberry blinking and studying him.

"I thought maybe you meant you'd cleaned out the upstairs rooms. Mistaking them for a storeroom. That wouldn't do, you know."

"Upstairs rooms?" Michael looked from Fiona to Gadberry and back again.

"There's a lovely little apartment upstairs that Mr. Gadberry has furnished in antiques." Fiona pointed one finger upward.

"It has an outside entrance," Gadberry told him, as if he suspected Michael was about to ask why he'd never seen any stairs leading to the alleged apartment. "Tried to talk Fiona into taking it when it first came open."

Devin strolled up to join them.

Gadberry gave a curt nod to the boy. "But the apartment's strictly a one-person arrangement. Perfect for someone to watch over the place and still have some privacy. If I could just find the right tenant."

Just then, the security guard poked his head through the front door. "Um, the radio wouldn't work, Mr. Gadberry. I guess I'll have to go back now and tell them everything is all clear here."

"Yes, you do that." Gadberry rolled his eyes. But before the door had finally fallen completely shut, he leaned back and called after the departing man, "And while you're at it, tell them that I'm finding a new security service."

The door closed with a scraping *thud*.

Gadberry folded his arms. "Fool operation—took them more than half an hour to respond to the news that someone saw lights on inside the shop. Then the fellow shows up, and his radio doesn't even work. Makes me wish, now more than ever, that I could rent out the upstairs to a—"

Michael cleared his throat.

Fiona's gaze swung to his, her eyes narrowing.

Michael patted her arm. She might not like the idea of his living right over her place of work, but it certainly met all his needs. It was already furnished, close to work, and most of all, close to Fiona. He couldn't have asked for a better arrangement.

Gadberry beat him to the punch. "Where do you live, young man?"

"Actually, I've been staying in a motel across the river until I can find a more permanent place."

"Excellent." The older man nodded. "And have you any experience beyond retail sales?"

"I was a private security guard for an apartment complex."

"Good. Very good." Gadberry stretched out the *very*, then honed his gaze in on Michael. "Could you get me references?"

Michael thought of Benny's offer. "Yes, I could. But there is one thing you should know about me before this discussion goes any further, Mr. Gadberry."

"What's that?" Gadberry lifted his chins and peered down his ski-slope nose at Michael. "That you're the fellow who caused all that ruckus over some Irish gold?"

"You know?" It surprised Michael and put him on alert at the same time.

"I wouldn't have approved your hiring if I didn't know something about your record. A good businessman doesn't get slipshod at hiring time. He checks references, makes calls, learns whatever he can about the people he's going to entrust with his goods and his good name."

"I told him," Fiona whispered from the corner of her mouth.

Michael nodded. He'd already had a good idea that she was the brains—and apparently sometimes the conscience—of Gadabout Gifts.

"But that doesn't mean I approve of this plan, Michael. In fact, I think it's a very bad plan. A bad plan indeed."

The coolness returned to her voice, tension to her posture, doubt to her eyes.

"I understand no charges were brought against you," Gadberry said. "Is that right?"

None by the law, he wanted to say. Though Fiona's eyes charged him time and again just as they were doing right now. "No, sir, no charges."

"Then I don't see the problem. If you've been honest and produce a good reference, I can even make it into a working proposition. You're a part-time employee here, aren't you?"

"Twenty hours a week," Fiona informed him.

"Twenty hours, minimum wage." Gadberry let out a snort of disgust. "What do you say to this: I give you the apartment and a small salary in exchange for your keeping an eye on things around here when we're closed up—in addition to your regular pay and duties. Sound fair?"

"Quite fair, Mr. Gadberry."

"I guess that depends on where you're standing," Fiona muttered, her arms crossed, leaving no doubt as to her feelings on the matter.

What now, Lord? Michael made a quick, silent prayer. *Do I take what seems the perfect solution to all my problems, knowing it could well hurt and disappoint Fiona again?*

His gaze fell on her face, the pain settled so deep in her eyes someone else might never notice it. His questions dissolved.

"I'm sorry, Mr. Gadberry. Much as I'd like that apartment, I can't and I won't. But thank you for the asking."

Five

"Are you kidding?" Devin punched Michael in the shoulder. "How can you turn down a deal like that?"

"Devin, this doesn't concern you." Fiona's pulse quickened. Her dead-on gaze willed Devin not to press the issue. She and Michael would not spend any more time together than necessary. Though she'd almost forgotten why it mattered so much to her, something deep inside her knew she just wasn't ready—not ready to risk, not ready to trust, not ready to forgive.

Despite her love for her son, she would not let Devin push things between her and Michael faster than she could manage.

"Your Uncle Mike declined the apartment. Leave it at that."

"But, Mom, it doesn't make any sense," Devin protested.

"Devin, don't argue with your mother over this." Michael's voice was steady and quiet.

Fiona tried not to think about how good it felt to have him lend support to her position.

"What's with you two?" Devin turned to Michael. "Uncle Mike, you need a place to stay, and a guy can't make a living with just a part-time job, especially while paying rent at some motel."

"Well, it's not exactly a four-star establishment, son." *Son.* Michael's use of the term came so subtly that no one but Fiona even appeared to notice it.

"Hey, four-star or four-walls-and-a-cot, they still charge money for it. Maybe I'm just barely passing math, but I can figure out that paying *some* rent is more than paying *no* rent."

"Just barely passing math, you say?" Concern colored Michael's voice. "Last year, when I was working with you, you brought home a solid B average."

"So he's slipped a little," Fiona snapped. She squared her shoulders, feeling defensive on behalf of her child. "Devin has been through an awful lot this semester, in case you've forgotten."

"No, I haven't forgotten," Michael murmured. He ducked his head but kept his gaze on hers.

Mr. Gadberry folded his arms and shifted his weight, not bothering to hide his curiosity in the conversation.

Fiona swiped her palm over her shirt and shut her eyes, her jaw clenched, as if that would help her order her conflicting thoughts about this situation.

In their youth, Michael had been a bright student who had managed to stay in school despite the lack of support from his father. He had loved learning and could often be found with his nose buried in a book—when he wasn't up to some mischief, that is. Many said it was Michael's mastery of math and science that made his jewelry so exquisite—because he had such an eye for balance, detail, and precision.

Under his tutelage, Devin had begun to make serious strides in school. Fiona had felt great pride in her son's improvements. She also felt true happiness in seeing Devin pleased with his own ability to comprehend and do the work, and in the way that translated into greater self-confidence.

She had Michael to thank for that. But then, she also had Michael to thank for Devin's falling so far behind.

"Devin will catch up on his school work in summer school," she said, sounding more sure than she felt.

"Aw, Mom."

"Spare me that tone of voice, young man." She folded her

arms. "You are going to summer school and that's that. Just as your Uncle Mike is not going to take the apartment. Both are settled, and there's no use discussing it further."

Devin folded his arms, too. "Not even If I promise that if he moves in here, I'll come down after school so he can help me with my homework?"

Devin's plan had its appeal. She threw a sidelong glance at Michael, who leaned back and, saying nothing, slowly crossed his arms over his chest as well. Yes, she admitted grudgingly, Devin needed the help, and it would be a comfort to know that her son was safe with Michael while she was working.

"Don't you see it, Mom? Uncle Mike taking that apartment is perfect." Devin's green eyes went into a long, exaggerated roll, just in case everyone didn't already know that he thought her position absolutely ridiculous.

"I'm with the boy on this one," Gadberry chimed in. "It certainly seems the ideal solution. For you as well as for me."

Fiona scowled. She didn't want it to look as though she'd caved in under the coercion of her son and her boss.

Unfazed, Gadberry turned to Michael to make his case. "It's so very simple. I need a night watchman, and you…"

He motioned the other man to fill in the rest.

"Have been a night watchman." Michael said.

"You need an apartment?…"

Michael glanced at Fiona.

She held her breath. The overhead light seemed more garish than usual in contrast to the deep hue of the night sky out the shop window. It cast shadows beneath his clear, kind eyes. Tonight she saw no roguish glint, no ulterior motive lurking just beneath the surface. Only Michael, the man she had once loved enough to want to marry, once trusted as a true friend. Could she trust him again?

"You need an apartment, and..." Gadberry said again.

Michael gave her a helpless shrug, then gave Gadberry's answer with a sigh. "And you have an apartment."

"You need more than part-time work?..." Gadberry's cheeks puffed as he continued the line of reasoning.

"I get where you're going, sir, and I do appreciate the suggestion, but the answer is still—"

The fact that Michael would turn down the very thing he needed most right now, and all for her, nudged the scales in his favor. She could trust him; she knew that. Fiona placed her hand on Michael's arm. "He'll take them—the job and the apartment."

"Where do you want this box, Uncle Mike?"

Fiona watched Michael crane his neck to read the upside-down words *Handle with Care* and *This Side Up* scrawled in his own handwriting on the cardboard box that Devin was holding.

"Here." He took two quick steps to reach the boy. "Let me take that for you, son."

Devin hoisted the box into Michael's arms.

Chink. Chink. Something small and metallic clattered as Michael ever so gently righted the package. He grimaced at the sound as Devin, oblivious to the problem, loped off to get another load.

Fiona looked up from the hamper full of the folded clothes she'd been tucking away in drawers. "Oh, Michael, I hope that wasn't something—"

Ka-chink.

"Breakable." She winced.

"It's fine." He carefully set down the box and patted it a few times. "Don't worry about this. 'Tis just some old jewelers' things, nothing of any importance."

"What do you mean, nothing of any importance?" She studied his calm expression, expecting him to offer further explanation.

Michael responded with an awkward shrug.

The stinging scent of pine cleaner and the unmaskable odor of the aging building filled her nostrils. She waited.

A week had passed since she'd agreed that it made sense for him to take this apartment and Gadberry's offer to work as a night watchman for the shop. During that time she had scarcely seen Michael and had offered to help with his move only because she felt she needed the closure. She needed to see this to the end, to see him settled in his new life so that she could move on with hers.

After today, they would go their separate ways, as much as their close proximity and working conditions allowed, and things would settle into a quiet, controlled routine. Unless, of course, something happened to change her thinking—Michael's returning to his once-loved craft, for instance.

"So it's a few of my old things in this box." He frowned. "What is it you're getting at, Fiona?"

"Michael, those are your jewelers' tools." The statement rang of accusation, which she backed up with a stony glare.

"That and a few pieces I've done over the years, yes."

"A few pieces?" She sidestepped the box of clothes. "You mean you're still making—"

"No." The warm glow of the light over his head did nothing to thaw the chill in his features.

"But you just said you had some pieces, and you've kept your tools. That must mean—"

"Not 'no' to the jewelry making, 'no' to the whole direction

73

of the conversation." He cocked his head, and the red high-lights winked in his deep auburn hair.

Standing in his new home, against the backdrop of decades-old wallpaper and Gadberry's antiques, he seemed imposing indeed. His broad shoulders blotted out much of the doorway behind him, and his powerful build was a sharp contrast to the delicate carved furniture and ornate knickknacks all about. The sight drove home her image of him as a man caught between the present and the past.

Looking at Michael Shaughnessy and seeing in him both the man she had loved and the man she was afraid to wholly trust suddenly gave her a full understanding of his predicament. And it made her all the more ready to finish up here and go back to her own quiet, safe apartment.

"I'd best be getting back to the unpacking then." She turned on her heel. "Forget that I even asked about the jewelry."

"What jewelry?" Devin bounded into the room.

"Put that suitcase over there." Fiona pointed to the chest of drawers, hoping to derail the boy's curiosity. "Then go back and get another load, please."

"There aren't any other loads. This is the last of everything." Devin clunked the suitcase down where he'd been told. He slapped his hands together, turned to Michael, and grinned. "What jewelry?"

"None of your never-mind, young man," Fiona said. "Now why don't you scoot yourself off to the kitchen to unload the groceries so we can be done here and get home in time to make some supper?" She shooed him in the direction of the kitchen with both hands.

"We didn't bring any groceries in, Mom." Devin folded his arms over his chest, his oversized feet planted firmly on the faded floral carpet.

74

"No groceries?" She clicked her tongue at Michael, grateful for the change of subject. "What are you going to do for dinner tonight?"

"Well, I—"

"You're not fooling me, Mom," Devin interrupted before Michael could reply. "Uncle Mike has fed himself just fine without your help for a lot of years so far. Why the sudden concern now? Unless, of course, you're trying to throw me off the trail."

"Trail? There is no trail, Devin, but if your Uncle Mike doesn't have anything to eat, then maybe we should—"

"Invite him to dinner? Great idea, Mom. Problem solved. Now, about this jewelry you're trying to hide from me—"

"Oh, Devin." Fiona sighed. "Not including you in a discussion that is clearly none of your business is not the same thing as hiding things from you."

"Let me guess." He stole a peek at his mother, then at Michael, an impish grin on his face. "You found some antique jewelry up here in a floor vent or something, didn't you? And now you're wondering if you should turn it in to the police or demand that Gadberry give you a solid explanation."

Fiona gave an exaggerated groan. "The only thing I am wondering, young man, is what I did to deserve you and that Irish imagination of yours."

"Maybe the fact that you were born Irish yourself?" Devin suggested. The twinkle in his eyes showed his joy in teasing her as he fell into a thick and sweetly familiar brogue. "Now had you had the good sense to be born in, oh, say Cleveland, you'd have been spared the agony o' havin' an Irish son with an Irish imagination—and you'd know how to do the polka on top of it all!"

Devin stepped toward her, his arms open as if to sweep her up into a clomping version of the dance right there and then.

Fiona raised her hands and looked heavenward, playing along. "Lord, save me from my son's reasoning. And from the polka, while you're at it."

"So, I've worn you down then, and you're going to tell me what jewelry it is you're talking about?"

"I'd rather do the polka." She narrowed one eye at him in challenge.

"Stop it now, you two, before this gets really ugly," Michael finally said, chuckling. "If you must know, Devin, this box contains my tools and some pieces of the jewelry I've crafted over these past few years."

"Jewelry?" If Michael had said he knew how to juggle live squid, Devin's expression couldn't have been more perplexed. "You can make jewelry?"

"I can and I do—that is, I did. It's the craft of my family. I began learning it when I was about your age." He paused and stuffed his hands into his pockets. "I guess your mother has never shown you her ring, then?"

The mention of the ring, the promise of a heart given and accepted, made Fiona flinch. She swallowed hard and tucked a strand of hair behind her ear.

"We'd better finish up here. It's getting late." Fiona moved back to the task of putting clothes away.

"I can do the rest, Fiona." Michael took a few strides to stand before her.

"Nonsense, Michael, we offered our help, and we'll stay until the job is done." She reached down to pick up a soft gray sweater from the hamper only to find her hands colliding with Michael's.

They both looked up.

Fiona's pulse thudded in her ears. Her throat went dry as she felt her lips open. No words came out.

"I don't want you to stay from a sense of duty, Fiona." The tips of Michael's fingers brushed her knuckles.

The hair on the back of her neck pricked up.

He slipped the sweater from her hands. "But I do want you to stay."

A tingle of warmth spread across her cheeks. She imagined the glow there looked as subtle as the embers of a fire.

"I…" Fiona blinked.

Had she taken leave of all her senses? This man had not long ago plunged her into a world of fear and anxiety. He'd chosen a pot of legendary gold over her, her feelings, and even her family—and he'd done it twice.

And now she stood in his apartment staring up at him all moon eyed and weak kneed. And why? Because he seemed so much like the boy she'd once loved? She shook her head as if that would adjust her thinking.

"No, Michael, maybe I shouldn't stay—if you can handle the rest yourself."

"Of course I can." He stepped away from her. "You do what you think best, Fiona."

She kept her gaze fixed on his. "Come on, then, Devin, we've got to be going on home."

"Now?"

She jerked her head around so fast that a red curl fell across one eye. She batted it away and tipped her head up. "Yes, *now.* Let's leave your Uncle Mike to get settled in without our inter-ference."

She snagged Devin by the arm and began hauling him toward the front door.

The boy stumbled along behind her. "But what about—"

Michael gave a stiff wave. "I can take care of it from here, son."

"Good-bye, Michael." Fiona moved outside in a rush, without even looking back.

"Good-bye," Michael said, then added to Devin, "I'll be fine."

"Okay, if you say so." Devin paused in the doorway to lift his hand in farewell. "Guess we'll see you in a couple hours, then, Uncle Mike."

"What?" She and Michael voiced their surprise in unison.

"At dinner," Devin said, as if they were daft for not recalling his suggestion.

"Oh, we never—" Fiona fumbled with the neckline of her shirt.

"I'm afraid I can't—" Michael cleared his throat.

"What is wrong with you two?"

"Nothing. Nothing is wrong." Fiona forced a light laugh. "Not a thing."

"We're fine," Michael confirmed.

Devin made a face at their overly enthusiastic insistence. "Then we'll see you in a couple hours, Uncle Mike."

He went hurtling down the stairs.

Fiona made an apologetic shrug.

"If you don't want me to come—" Michael leaned against the door frame.

"Oh no, you don't."

"Don't what?"

"Leave me to explain everything to Devin on my own. You're coming to dinner tonight, Michael Shaughnessy, and that is that."

"That was delicious, Fiona." Michael folded his linen napkin on the table beside his empty plate. "I haven't had anything so good since—"

Fiona visibly tensed. She twisted her napkin in both hands just above the half-eaten bowl of stew before her.

Michael cleared his throat. He traced one fingertip along the smooth fabric of the tablecloth.

Her near-frantic expression pleaded in silence with him, but for what, he wondered. She obviously did not want him dredging up the past—but which one? The long ago past of Ireland and their ill-fated love, or the recent past when he'd been welcome in this home? Both memories made his heart clench and his breath stop short in his lungs.

He clenched his teeth. "I haven't had anything this good in a long while."

She laid her napkin aside and dipped her head with a murmured thank-you.

Michael nodded.

Fiona picked up her spoon, stared down into the rich stew, then laid her spoon aside again.

Michael glanced around the room, hoping for something to catch his attention so he could begin a new conversation.

Across the table from him, Devin tipped his bowl up, scraped his spoon across the bottom of it, and slurped up the last of his stew with gusto.

"Devin, really." Fiona shook her head at her son.

He grinned back at her.

Michael chuckled. He hadn't seen Devin grin like that in a long time.

"It's all right." Michael reached out to pat Fiona's hand. "'Tis just the boy's way of complimenting your fine cooking, darlin' girl."

Her gaze fell to his touch on her skin, and when he spoke the tender term that sometimes slipped out without his thinking, a slow blush crept across her creamy cheeks. It had been too long since he'd seen Fiona react so.

He drew in a deep breath to savor the God-is-good feeling that filled him with gratitude for all the blessings given to one so undeserving.

Fiona lifted her eyes to meet his gaze from beneath the fringe of her lashes.

Michael kept his hand on hers, his pulse registering hard but steady in his ears. Was this a sign that she had accepted him as her friend again—and that she might even be able to forgive him for all the pain he'd inflicted on her? If only he could be sure.

As if she knew he needed more from her, she bit her lower lip, paused, then curled her fingers around his hand and gave it a squeeze.

He returned the gesture.

Fiona smiled.

Michael's heart soared. After everything he'd done, she could forgive him; he knew it now. He took her hand more firmly in his and covered it with his other hand, wishing this feeling could last indefinitely.

Devin's chair slid back over the floor with a grinding squawk. The boy stood, stretched his gangly arms toward the ceiling, then placed his palms on the table and asked, "So, Mom, why don't you show me this ring Uncle Mike was talking about?"

Fiona pulled her hand from Michael's as quickly as a blade drawn from a sheath.

He wanted to reach after her, to regain the moment, but he knew it had passed. He heaved a weary sigh and ran one hand back through his hair. "Maybe that's best left to another time, Devin."

After all, Michael thought, bringing it up now would only

embarrass Fiona and bring more distance between the two of them. The memories of the time they had shared in their youth and of how they'd parted could only reopen old hurts and disappointments just when Michael felt she might be ready to move past the new hurt and disappointment he'd caused her. That was the last thing he wanted.

"Actually, Michael," Fiona said as she pushed back her chair and stood, "I think I'd like to show Devin the ring. It would be a good lesson to him."

"But, Fiona—"

She held her hand up. "I haven't taken it out to look at in a very long time, and I think I'd like to see it again." She paused. "And you could do with a peek at it yourself."

"Me? Why do I need to see it again?"

"As a reminder."

He was afraid of that.

"A reminder of what, Mom?" Devin followed on his mother's heels like an eager pup as she walked out of the room.

"When you see it, you'll understand, son," she said, her voice clear and loud enough to ensure Michael would hear. "The lovely ring your Uncle Mike once gave to me was made by his own hands. It will be a good thing to take it out again and let it serve as a reminder—"

Michael hung his head, his fine spirits dashed as he heard the next words.

"Of all the things that once were, or all that might have been—and all the things that never change."

S i x

I t's called a Claddagh ring, son. I'm sure you've seen its design before." Fiona, a small red box in her hand, led the way back to the dining table where Michael waited.

When they entered the room, Michael leaned back in his chair and frowned.

Fiona tried to imagine how he must feel to see her parading out the familiar ring. He'd told her just today that he had no interest in even talking about his talent, his craft, or his creations. Now, to have her force that very issue by showing Devin his workmanship—

She stole a glance at his darkened features. "Um, Michael, why don't you tell a bit of its history?"

"History?"

"Yes, of the Claddagh ring." She set the unopened box on the table as she settled into the chair next to his. "Maybe if you told Devin something about it?"

His brows angled down.

Devin grabbed a chair by the back and swung it around on one leg so that it rested right beside Fiona. Straddling the seat, he leaned his chin on both hands and gazed expectantly at Michael.

"I don't know what it is you want me to tell, Fiona."

"You know," she urged. "About how the ring's design is a hundred years old and—"

"Three hundred."

"What?"

"The design is over *three* hundred years old."

"You tell it, Michael. You'll do it so much better than I could." Fiona pressed her lips together and stole a peek at Devin.

Her son's full attention was on Michael.

"This ring…" He reached out to pluck the box from the table and held it up, still tightly shut, for effect. "The Claddagh is a tradition in western Ireland dating back for centuries. Its roots go back to the tiny fishing village of Claddagh, just outside the walls of Galway."

His hushed tones infused with the rolling lilt of his brogue made the simple statement sound like the "once upon a time" of a fairy tale.

"Do you remember Ireland well, Devin?" Michael cocked his head. "The grass so green and the sea, gray into the horizon with whitecaps strewn across its mighty waves?"

The boy nodded. "I remember."

"And the fine traditions passed down from one generation to the next?"

"And the family stories," Devin said.

Both Fiona and Michael stiffened.

Michael, leaning forward to rest his elbows on his thighs, steered the talk away from a painful subject. "I'm glad to know you remember your homeland, son. But I hope it doesn't stop at memories. I hope you always learn more and cherish what you learn about our people and their ways.

"The Claddagh is a very old tradition." Slowly, Michael lifted the top of the box, its hinges squeaking in the quiet. "Have you seen its design before?"

"Yeah." Devin pinched the ring between his fingers and wriggled it loose from the satin cushion. "I've seen it before, but I never knew anything about it."

He turned it this way and that. The light over the dining table made the warm gold gleam.

Fiona's teeth sank into her lower lip. She reached toward the piece, but before she could take it, Michael held his hand out, and Devin dropped the ring into his open palm. She drew in a sharp breath but said nothing.

She had not looked at the ring in years, though she had never been able to part with it. Long ago, she had convinced herself that was because it represented her youth and Michael's talent, not because of what it had once meant to them both. And so she felt completely unprepared for the emotional impact she now felt at seeing the ring she'd once worn.

Tears filled her eyes but did not fall. She swallowed hard, but the cold lump in her throat remained. This was supposed to be about Michael and showing him the way back to his God-given talent, not about their painful past. She had to make herself believe that.

She could make herself believe it, she thought, and hiked her chin up, defying the burning threat of tears in her eyes and the tightness in her chest. She'd taken the ring out to force Michael to confront his own potential, and that was it.

When Michael picked up the ring, she simply stopped breathing.

"It's really neat, Uncle Mike." Devin squinted as he looked at the ring from all angles. "Does it have a special meaning?"

Fiona tried to compel Michael's gaze to meet hers, to no avail. Her lungs ached as she drew in the mingled aromas of dinner, the dust from the old jewelry box, and Michael's after-shave, which she had suddenly become aware of.

Michael rubbed the tip of his thumb over the ring as he studied it. "Each part of the design has a meaning, son. See the crown here?" He traced the rounded top of the crown with his thumbnail.

"Uh-huh."

"That symbolizes fidelity. And the clasped hands, friendship."

"And the heart?" Devin asked.

"Well, what do *you* suppose a heart would symbolize?"

"Love?"

"Yes, my boy, that's right." Michael slowly lifted his gaze
from the ring to find Fiona's eyes.

He did not smile. His eyes held no mischief. He wasn't sad,
either, but solemn and perhaps a bit wistful when he closed his
hand over the ring and nodded. "Yes, the heart symbolizes love
everlasting."

She blinked. Despite her vow that this discussion would be
about Michael's craft, dampness thickened her lashes, and her
nose tingled. But she did not cry.

"So, just what is it, Uncle Mike?" Devin sat up, his arms
braced straight against the back of the chair. "Is it a friendship
ring or more serious than that?"

"Well, that all depends, son." A strained, husky quality
deepened Michael's voice.

"Depends on what?"

"Here, let me show you." Michael took Fiona's left hand and
drew it toward him.

Sensing what he had in mind, she tried to tug her fingers
free, but he held tight. She pulled her shoulders back, her eyes
narrowed at him.

He smiled, just a ghost of a smile.

She scowled.

He tipped his chin down.

This was about your going back to making jewelry, she wanted
to scold him, *nothing more.*

But with her hand in his, she knew it *was* about more.

One fleeting sidelong glance at Devin assured her he saw

nothing more to this than a lesson in an old Irish custom. That gave her some relief. No matter what the ring had meant or what it might mean to them now, her son was only thinking of it as a quaint bit of family history.

And she could use Devin's curiosity to encourage Michael to talk about his talent. That would be good for Michael and would steer the conversation clear of their past, as well.

Her shoulders relaxed just a bit. She fixed her gaze on Michael's once again.

Please, his eyes seemed to say. *Trust me.*

Yes, she felt sure that was what he was asking. If she made this show of trust, she would be letting him know that all ties between them were not severed, giving him hope.

He held the ring up.

But hope for what? Hope of friendship or of more? She decided to use the Claddagh to give him her answer.

Fiona stretched her *right* hand out to Michael.

He gave her a wink.

"Now, you see, Devin," Michael began, brandishing the ring with a flourish, "it's all in how the ring is worn."

Devin scooted close to observe.

"When a man gives a woman the ring, it's a symbol of affection. Slip it on the right hand with the heart turned outward, so." Michael demonstrated on Fiona's finger. "And that says to the world, 'my heart has not yet been won.'"

"Uh-huh."

"But turn it with the heart inward…" Michael hesitated.

Fiona gently drew her hand away.

Michael looked at her, his eyes filled with understanding, but a touch of sorrow as well.

"Worn with the heart inward is the wearer's way of proclaiming her heart is taken."

For a moment, Fiona felt transported back to the day he had first given her the ring. She'd known such happiness, such pride, that the man she cared for with all her heart had made the gift with his own hands. She'd worn it that day with the heart turned inward, to let him know she loved him but was not yet ready for a deeper pledge.

She saw in his face, in his posture, that he remembered, too.

"Is that all?" Devin's impatient tone intruded on the silence.

"Hmm?"

Fiona prompted Michael with a toe to his shin.

"Oh, um, no. No, there's another meaning for the ring," he explained, folding his hands in his lap. "Worn on the left hand, heart inward, it becomes an engagement ring or even a wedding ring because it symbolizes a promise of two hearts given to each other—"

Fiona touched the ring, her breath caught in anticipation.

"Forever," Michael concluded.

"Wow." Devin folded his spindly arms around his ribs. "That's pretty cool."

Michael grinned, obviously pleased with the reaction. "Yes, I suppose it is."

"But, you know, it really is kind of hard to believe." The boy, not a practiced actor, scratched his head to suggest how perplexed he was. "That is, you think you know someone and then you learn something about them that really surprises you. Why didn't you tell me this before?"

Fiona heaved a sigh of relief. Here it was. Finally, they'd get to the heart of the matter, the whole reason she'd broken down and trotted out the ring.

She squirmed in her seat, her arms laced over her chest and her head tipped up.

"What are you talking about, Devin?" Michael folded his own arms. There the three of them sat, mirror images of one another, all waiting for the other shoe to drop. "Why didn't I tell you *what* before?"

Fiona stuck out her hand and tapped the ring with one finger as if to celebrate her genius in getting Michael to deal with the gift he had turned his back on years ago. She all but hummed her satisfaction.

Devin narrowed one eye, first at Michael, then at her, and demanded, "Why didn't you guys tell me that you two were once engaged?"

Fiona's jaw dropped.

"It wasn't an engagement in the way you're thinking, Devin." Michael glanced at Fiona, letting her expression and body language guide him as to how much or how little to tell.

They'd moved into the living room to get more comfortable. Yet somehow comfort was not the word that sprang to mind when Michael shifted in the lone wing chair while Fiona and Devin fidgeted on the nearby couch. He'd tried to excuse himself, to allow Fiona to handle Devin's questions as she saw fit, and that wasn't just because he'd made a significant breakthrough with her today and wanted to get out before something happened to undo it. However, after a pointed look from Fiona and some ribbing from Devin, he realized he had to stay.

He watched Fiona twist the ring that still circled her slender finger. A swell of pride and relief filled his heart.

Yes, he did hope to be on his way before the delicate balance tipped from his favor, but he also wanted to give Fiona and Devin some privacy. It wasn't his place, he felt, to impose on this family matter. Fiona apparently disagreed, he guessed, as she gestured with a rolling wave of her hand for him to go on with what he was saying.

"Your mother and I never set a wedding date, Devin. I never even had the chance to ask your grandfather for the darlin' girl's hand."

"But you gave her a ring. No, you *made* her a ring. That sounds pretty serious to me."

"Well, yes, I did make her a ring. But then, that was my trade at the time, son. If I'd studied with a glassmaker, she might have gotten a set of crystal goblets."

Fiona rolled her eyes.

Devin shared her opinion with a *harrumph.* "C'mon, Uncle Mike. Giving a girl a ring is way more serious than giving her goblets, and you know it."

"We were young." Michael cleared his throat. "The world seemed full of promise, and we…we were young."

"You said that."

"Well, it's true. Your mother was only eighteen and I not much more than that. I asked her to wear my ring, but she wisely never moved it to her left hand." He folded his hands. The discussion seemed to be going well so far; he was serving out just enough information without touching on the rift that had come between him and Fiona. "Then I chose not to try to make a living as a jewelry maker, and your mother realized I'd never be able to support a family without a trade; and we went our own ways, and then your father came courting and—"

He was rambling, and he had no idea how to shut himself up.

"What Uncle Mike is trying to say is…" Fiona leaped to his rescue, her hands outstretched as if to restrain him from stumbling on. "We were young, and while that doesn't mean our feelings weren't valid, there were so many other things to take into account. And all in all, 'twas the right decision not to marry."

Although he knew her meaning, it hurt Michael to hear her say the words, even all these years later.

"Because you met my father?" Devin asked.

"No, I didn't meet your father. That is, I don't recall ever not knowing your father—or your Uncle Mike or Uncle Cameron, for that matter." She smiled, pushing her hair back.

Curled up on the couch with her feet tucked beneath her, she didn't look much older than the young woman who had accepted his invitation to a church outing, their first date.

"But I never realized that your father cared for me until after I stopped wearing this ring...." Her voice trailed off. She held up her hand and gently moved her fingers so the light played off the golden band.

They fell into silence. Michael understood that both of them were reflecting on the loss of Neal, who had been husband, father, and friend, and who, despite his demanding nature, was sorely missed. He wished he knew what to say to sum up the emotions and realities in a way that would put them at ease. Perhaps this would be a good time to take his leave.

Before he could make his good-byes, the sharp chirp of the telephone pierced the quiet around them.

"Excuse me." Fiona jumped up and hurried off to the kitchen to take the call.

"I still have plenty to do back at my new apartment, Devin." Michael pushed up from the chair. "Maybe I'd better—"

"I just don't get it, Uncle Mike."

Even as the next words formed on his tongue, Michael wondered if he'd regret them. "Don't get what, Devin?"

"If you can make a ring as good as the one you gave Mom, then why would you work in a gift shop or do private security?"

He braced one foot against the coffee table and pressed back against the couch, almost as if issuing a challenge. "Have you forgotten how to do it?"

"No, I haven't forgotten."

"Then why did you stop?"

He knew of no way to talk about his drifting away from his craft without speaking of the gold and what his obsession had cost him. That seemed such tired ground now. It would only drag them backward when he wanted their relationship to move on.

Michael swiped his hand across his jaw then down his neck. "Let's just say there isn't much call for Claddagh rings in Cincinnati and leave it at that."

"Can't you learn how to make some other kind of ring? Or maybe a—"

"I know how to make many things, Devin. As a young man I was considered quite a craftsman and artist." His fingertips brushed over the chain around his neck, and he pulled the cross free. "I created this piece as well."

"Wow." Devin stood, his concentration fixed. "I've seen you wearing that before, but I never realized you made it."

"It was the first really fine piece I crafted—the first in gold." He let the chain drape over the back of his thumb, and the weight of the cross made it swing gently as Devin inspected it. "I worked and saved for a long time to afford the gold. I wanted this to be just right, to be more than a show of what I could do, but also as a sign of what was done for me."

Devin raised his eyes to Michael. "So your skill was also your testimony?"

He'd never thought of it that way. If he'd ever seen his talent as anything but an impossible way to make a living, he might have pursued it; it might have defined the kind of man he'd become. He had not wanted that. He had not wanted anything, whether love for Fiona or his talent for jewelry making or even his faith, to interfere with his one goal: to win back the gold and the honor his grandfather had lost.

Michael let the cross drop to his chest. "I'm afraid as testimonies go, it's been a pretty silent one. You know more than anyone that the way I've lived my life has spoken volumes more about my shortcomings than this one cross could say about my salvation."

"That's why we need the cross, though, isn't it?" Devin cocked his head as though he were thinking something through. "Because we're all full of shortcomings?"

"Yes, son."

A smile worked up from deep inside Michael, and he reached out to put his hand on Devin's shoulder. First Fiona and the ring, and now Devin and the necklace, had shown him the hope he needed. He finally felt he could believe that the relationships his actions had severed could be made whole again.

"So, are you ever going to make another one of those crosses?" Devin grinned.

"That a hint?"

"Well, if you did, and it just so happened to wind up in a box with my name on it, I wouldn't throw it in a drawer somewhere."

"Oh, now stop it." He gave the boy's shoulder a squeeze, playing along with the underwhelming show of interest from his godson. "You're turning my head with all your flattery, you are."

Devin threw a wide mock punch at Michael, obviously embarrassed by revealing so much of his spiritual self.

Michael, feeling energized by the hope that he hadn't

destroyed the bonds with Devin and Fiona, wrangled the boy into a feather-light headlock.

Devin countered with a jab to the ribs.

"What on earth are you two up to?" Fiona walked into the room at a brisk pace. "Honestly, I can't leave you alone for one minute."

"Aw, Mom, we were just kidding around." Devin straightened.

Michael stood and whisked his hand down his shirt. His knuckle brushed the cross lying on his chest. He started to tuck the piece away as was his habit, then paused and left it there in the open. "Actually, I was just telling Devin good-bye, Fiona. I still have unpacking to do."

"You're going?"

Was it his wishful thinking that made her sound disappointed? Could she actually want him to stay?

Michael tried to verify it in her face, but one look at those green eyes framed by wayward red curls, and he forgot his intent. He'd spent a whole evening with her, had made progress, and hadn't once heard mention of the gold or of the past that had broken her trust. Time to get going while the going was good, he told himself.

He nodded and took one step backward. "I have to get back to the apartment. Mr. Gadberry is counting on me to walk through the shop and storeroom each evening before I go to bed and to be available if there's a problem."

"He ought to get you a beeper."

"I'll tell him." Michael took another step back, his focus on the ring on Fiona's finger.

"And a cellular phone."

"Good idea." Another backward step, this time with a glance over his shoulder to see whether he was closing in on the door. "He's already investing in a closed-circuit security system for the shop. Anything else I should suggest?"

"How about a really cool, really fast car?" Devin suggested.

"I hardly need a fast car," Michael said, his eyebrow raised in mock reproach.

"Then can I have it?" The boy made motor sounds through his lips, his hands gripping an imaginary steering wheel.

"Well now, there's a frightening thought." Michael chuckled. "Good thing we still have a few years before we have to think about riding with this wild one behind the wheel."

"Count me out of that." Fiona shook her head, her tone light but her expression serious. "You'll be an old man before I get into a vehicle with you, young man. Mark my words."

"Aw, Mom, you won't stick to that. I'll bet on the very day I get my license, you'll let me have the keys."

"I'll tell you what you can have right now, young man—" Fiona put her hands on her hips.

"I know, I know, I can have a piece of your mind to feast on." He grinned at her.

Michael could see how hard she had to fight not to grin back.

"But if it's all the same to you, Mom, I'll just say thanks but no thanks. I'm already full from dinner."

"Fine. Then you can just march into your room and lay out your good clothes—tomorrow's church, you know."

The boy slumped his shoulders forward as if she'd just burdened him with the weight of the world, but he obeyed and shuffled off toward his room.

"It's an awful effort, I tell you, getting that boy to put on nice clothes."

Michael nodded, searching his brain for something else to say to ease himself into a good-bye. "Um, oh, speaking of clothes, that reminds me—I still have that sweatshirt you loaned me when we cleaned the storeroom."

She looked confused for just a moment, then opened her mouth in a silent 'oh' of recognition.

Michael resisted a smile at his own brilliance. With his statement, he'd found a way both to lay the groundwork for his leaving and to set up a way to see Fiona again soon. He stepped to the front door, grabbed the knob, and said, "Why don't I bring it into the shop Monday for you?"

"Don't bother." She leaned against the wall beside him. "It was just a sweatshirt Cameron left behind. You can return it to him yourself when he gets here."

"Here?" Michael went rigid. "Cameron is coming here?"

"He's stopping in Cincinnati to finish up with his work." Fiona said it like a woman breaking difficult news to a child, her voice soft and her expression one of controlled concern. "He's retired from Interpol, you know."

Michael hadn't known. Cameron had once been like a brother to him, and Michael had ambushed and betrayed the man, all for a chance to get his hands on the stolen gold. Just the mention of him made Michael's stomach tighten into a knot.

"So he's back from Ireland then?" he managed to ask.

"Yes, that was him on the phone." She placed her hand on his wrist with such tenderness that Michael scarcely felt her touch. All the old feelings he thought had passed churned to the surface. Now more than ever he wanted to be on his way, before talk of Cameron turned to talk of Michael's misdeeds— and of what caused them.

"I told him you had come to dinner, and he seemed genuinely pleased."

"He did?"

"Yes. In fact, he asked me to tell you that he wants to see you."

He could not meet her gaze. "I don't know why he would want to."

"He's your oldest and dearest friend, Michael, that's why." She gave his wrist a caress. "And he said he had something to give you."

Michael jerked his head up. "Something for me? Did he say what?"

"No." She pressed her lips together, looked away for a moment, then lifted her chin and returned her gaze to his. "But I did get the feeling it had something to do with your grandfathers and the stolen gold."

Seven

No."

"Absolutely not."

Michael and Fiona both shook their heads.

The morning sun poured in through the shop's windows. It reflected with a blinding glare over the countertops and caught the faceted crystals dangling from a lampshade, throwing tiny bits of rainbow around the room.

Fiona touched the heart on the ring she'd slipped on her finger two days ago, her shoulders drawn up. "I, for one, want nothing more to do with that stolen gold, Cameron Brennan O'Dea!"

Her brother-in-law chuckled beneath his breath, his eyes dancing.

Michael looked away. His jaw tensed. The tremendous struggle this situation unleashed brought a red tinge to the hollow of his cheeks.

Fiona wanted to reach out to touch his arm to offer support, but she stopped herself. This time, she thought, it was Michael who should reassure her. Twice before he had valued the gold over her and her feelings. Now Cameron had returned from Ireland, offering a gold coin to each of them as a token of their history, and she was tensely watching Michael's response.

Fiona shuddered. Talk of the gold, the Claddagh ring on her hand, Michael beside her—all called back memories of the first time she had asked Michael to choose between her and his lost treasure.

His voice came back to her from that day: *"The O'Deas hold the secret of where it is buried, but 'twas the Shaughnessys' legacy long before that, Fiona. If I could place my hands on a single one of those gold coins, I could prove it. And I won't rest until I can do just that."* She had often wondered how a single coin could prove anything, but she didn't ask, afraid that she wouldn't want to hear the answer.

Now Cameron had come back from Ireland to finally, after all these years, present Michael with one of those gold coins. Her mind could hardly hold the swimming thoughts, the doubts, the questions, as she held her breath and waited to see if he would, as he had twice before, choose the gold.

"I can't believe you'd even mention it, Cameron—that you'd bring even a few pieces of that gold here." Low and taut, Michael's voice barely rose above a whisper. "I want no part of it."

Fiona let out a long sigh of relief.

Cameron slapped his hand on Michael's back. "'Tis a reward, old friend. Simple as that. When I returned the gold, a reward was offered. I asked for a few of the coins. They aren't worth as much as you might think in cold, hard monetary value."

He reached into his pocket and pulled free a small cloth bag.

Fiona tried not to be obvious in her interest in both the bag and Michael's reaction.

Cameron worked two fingers inside the drawstring and gave a firm jerk. The top opened, and he paused to make it clear he was watching Michael, then turned the bag upside down.

Four gleaming gold coins rang like harsh bells **as they** bounced against one another and the countertop, then spun to a stop. About the size and thickness of a U.S. nickel, each coin had a nondescript profile on one side and Gaelic writing on the other. But instead of a nickel's smooth edges, the gold coins all had deep, evenly spaced notches around their perimeters. When the last one had stilled with a quiet metallic clink, Cameron tossed the bag down alongside the gold.

"All our lives we'd been led to believe these coins represented a vast fortune." Cameron placed a finger on one coin and flicked it over the counter's edge into his open hand. "In reality, three generations of Shaughnessy and O'Dea men have carried the burden of a treasure that in today's economy could hardly make a down payment on a home, much less buy back everything lost to us."

"It was about more than money, and you know it, Cameron." Michael locked gazes with the other man, ignoring the coins. "For me, it was never just material gain. It was a matter of family honor, of redeeming something denied my great-grandfather, grandfather, then my father and myself—even my children after me."

"What children, Michael?" Cameron fisted his fingers around the coin. "It's not family honor that's been denied. It's we ourselves who have been denied. First our grandfathers' freedom, then our fathers' dignity. Now the two of us, all for the sake of an old legend and a handful of coins, have denied ourselves friendship and the treasures of a home and family to love and to love us in return. At least my brother Neal had the sense not to forsake that."

Fiona bowed her head. She had loved Neal, and their marriage had been a good one, but it had not been completely spared the effects of the O'Deas' past. She wished she could say so now, but the exchange felt far too private between Michael and Cameron.

She bit her lip and watched as Cameron unfurled his fingers to reveal the coin.

"Take it, Michael," Cameron urged. "May it serve as a reminder of all it cost. It's not a trick. I'm keeping one of them myself." The coin in his palm winked in the sunlight. "Take it."

Michael folded his arms with a deceptively casual air, then cinched them tight over his blue T-shirt.

Cameron rocked back and forth in a gesture that suggested a swagger.

Fiona swallowed hard.

The tension between the three of them all but crackled like static electricity.

Cameron cleared his throat.

Fiona tucked her hair behind her ear.

Both of them watched Michael, waiting for some reaction.

Michael cocked his head. His gaze bore into Cameron's, but he said nothing.

The two men stood, almost identical in size, but in appearance they were as different as the paths they'd followed in life. Cameron, his hair a bright gold, had a broad face that easily broke into a smile and carried a hint of humor about him. Michael, his hair dark, his features angular, seemed always to bear a faraway touch of sorrow in his eyes.

Fiona loved them both like family—and Michael a wee bit more.

She blinked. What was that? Her heart thudded high in her chest, and she felt the heavy rhythm of her pulse in her temples. Her hand shot to her lips as if to seal in the wayward thought before it came blurting out of her mouth.

I love Michael a wee bit more than family.

In a split second, she acknowledged this as truth and understood the importance of his reaction to Cameron's offer.

"Take the coin, Michael. I've brought one for you and one for myself and one each for Fiona and Devin."

"No." Without thinking, Fiona retreated a step. "I don't want one."

"Have you lost your senses?" Michael shoved Cameron's open hand aside with enough force to fling the coin back onto the counter. "After all we've put one another through, after all I've done to hurt the three people who matter most to me in this world, why would any of us want that—that—thing as a reminder of it all?"

"Michael is right, Cameron. I can't bear the sight of those coins, much less want to own one."

Michael moved close to put his arm around Fiona's shoulders.

Now, in light of her emerging feelings for the man, the protective gesture took on new meaning for her. A quick, thrilling tingle swept over her skin at his touch. She shut her eyes to blot out the temptation to look up at him and let him see her emotions.

"It's a bad idea."

For an instant, Fiona thought that Michael must have read her thoughts and spoken aloud to warn her away from anything but friendship with him.

"Cameron, I do see the good of what you're doing. But I wonder if it will work the way you think it will." Michael shook his head.

"I don't understand," Fiona said softly.

"For so long, we've let this gold symbolize more than it could ever possibly be." Michael turned from her to Cameron. "Now you want each of us to hold it, to carry it with us as a reminder that it's only an object. Am I right?"

The familiar smile returned to Cameron's face. "It's not such a far-fetched idea. Many of us carry something with us to remind us of who we are—and of what we count as our real treasure."

Cameron dipped his fingers inside his shirt collar. Slowly a thin gold chain appeared, then snagged on the fabric. He gave a tug, and out fell a cross much like the one Michael wore but without any engraving.

Michael smiled. "You still have it after all these years."

"I don't wear it often, or at least I didn't." He gave Fiona a reassuring smile and a wink. "No crisis of faith, you understand. Gold jewelry just didn't fit in with my work."

"Then why wear it now?" Michael narrowed his eyes.

"'Cause I'm out of that line of work, for one." He raked one hand back through his hair. "And because I wanted to make a point to you, old friend."

"That point wouldn't happen to be something along the lines of 'where your treasure is, there your heart will be also'?"

Fiona tilted her head. "Is that—"

"You'll find it in the Gospel of Matthew," Michael said, his eyes on Cameron. "It happens to be something I've been thinking about a lot lately—among other things."

Cameron leaned back against the counter. "I'd hate to sound patronizing, but..."

"Go ahead."

"It's good to hear you've been doing some soul-searching, friend. I always knew you were better than your recent behavior indicated."

"I knew it, too." Fiona dared give Michael a hug, happy that this business of the gold was now behind them.

Now that Michael had turned down even the single coin he'd said could prove his family's claims beyond any doubt, Fiona could face the future. Perhaps, she thought, wriggling her fingers to make her ring shine in the morning light, she and Michael could face the future—together.

"Well, I thank you both for the vote of confidence," Michael said. "And in light of all that's been said today, I have a suggestion for the gold."

"You do?" Fiona asked, expecting full well he'd say they should give it to charity, or even that Cameron should keep it.

"Yes, I do." He brushed one knuckle over her cheek. "And I think you'll be pleased."

Her heart swelled with newfound joy as she gazed at the man she now trusted not to put even one coin before her and her son. She put her hand on his.

"Cameron has already said he's keeping one coin for himself. And I don't think it's fair for me to do anything with Devin's except put it away for him until he's grown," she told him. "But whatever you wish to do with your coin, Michael, I'll add my own to it."

"Thank you, darlin' girl." Michael planted a kiss on her temple, then extended his hand to Cameron.

Fiona's brave heart plummeted, her hopes and assurances dashed when Michael opened his mouth, grinned at his friend, and said, "I've been waiting a long time for an opportunity like this, and I think it's long overdue. I'll take both coins."

"Well, that's it then. There's no changing it." Fiona slumped down in the wing chair, refolding a single sheet of paper along its two sharp creases. "Devin, the teacher says you'll not pass math this semester. You'll have to go to summer school to make it up."

"I'm sorry, Mom." The boy hung his head. "I tried to do the work, really I did. But I just couldn't get it. Then I got behind when—"

She held her hand up. Fiona knew full well when Devin fell irrevocably behind—when Michael took him away, keeping her son as a bargaining chip to get his hands on the gold coins.

Well, Michael had his coins now. Not the whole cache of them, but more than the one he'd sworn he needed to verify his family's story of stolen property. She hoped the coins would give him some comfort.

However, Fiona had her own problems concerning the coins—or coin, to be precise. She'd put away the last coin for Devin to have when he was older. She hadn't told him about it for his own good. But keeping this secret from her son played on her guilt, no matter how justified her decision might be.

Still, she believed she'd done the right thing. That gold had caused enough trouble for her family already. She would not inflict further harm on Devin by letting him know a piece of the legendary treasure lay in the locked safe at the shop.

She twisted her neck to study Devin over her shoulder. She had to be both father and mother to the boy now, and her every judgment concerning him weighed doubly heavy on her heart.

Yes, she had her own problems to deal with, all right, and they no longer concerned Michael Shaughnessy in any way, shape, or form.

"I'll do better in summer school, Mom." Devin leaned over the back of her chair. "Especially now that I have a private tutor again."

"You do?" She laid her head back and looked up at him.

"Duh, Mom." If he could have rolled his eyes back entirely inside his head, he would surely have done it then. "Have you completely forgotten about Uncle Mike?"

The fabric on the arms of the chair scrubbed against her palms as she shut her eyes and exhaled between clenched teeth. "No, I most certainly have *not* forgotten about Uncle Mike. I wish you would forget about him, however, because there is no way I want him to teach you anything."

"Why not?"

The reasons raced through her mind, making her stomach tighten. She couldn't explain it all to Devin right now, not in her current frame of mind, and not without revealing too much about Cameron's gift of the coins. Maybe later, she thought, after she had time to adjust to the fact that Michael had let her down one more time.

Sighing, she flicked at an imaginary speck on her jeans and said, "Let's just say that the things that man believes in are not the kinds of things I want you to learn."

"About math?"

"What?"

"He'd be working with me on math, Mom. You can't tell me he believes in some weird mathematical theory that I shouldn't learn about."

She tried not to smile too much at the boy's defensive sarcasm on Michael's behalf. If only it weren't so misplaced. "No, of course not."

"And you can't tell me that I didn't do much better in math when Uncle Mike was working with me."

She grew more sober. Her son had a point. "Yes, that's true."

"He's already volunteered to help. I need the help. He can tutor me in his apartment right over where you'll be working." Devin came around the side of the chair, then squatted beside her. "I just don't see what the big problem is."

It was the gold. But she knew no way of telling him that Michael had taken the pieces of gold and of her fears of what he might do with them without confessing she had one of the coins in her care. She just did not have the heart to do that—

not knowing as she did all the harm that the gold had wrought. To place it in the hands of her only child now, when he was still so young, so impressionable, would be irresponsible at best.

"Why, Mom? Why can't Uncle Mike help me with math?"

Fiona shook her head. "Fine. Ask him for help, but please just don't be too upset if things don't work out as well as you think they will."

It was the perfect solution. Michael worked the small box out of his jeans pocket.

Make use of the coins. Apply his talent. Find a way to express his desire to make amends to both Fiona and Devin, to show Fiona he'd changed. With one gesture, he'd found a way to do it all.

Now he'd come to present his gift to Devin. Once he'd done that, the legend of the gold, his journey back to his faith, and the reclaiming of his craft would all be complete. It made his spirit light just to think of how the boy would react when he saw the gift Michael had fashioned for him.

He pried open the hinged box with his thumb to admire the first truly unique piece of jewelry he'd designed and crafted in years. Snatching up the hem of his polo-style shirt, he rubbed at the gold until it glowed.

"Yes, who is it?" Fiona called out from behind her apartment door in reply to Michael's vigorous knocking moments before.

He snapped the box shut, then tucked it away again.

"It's me—Michael."

Silence.

A frown tugged at his mouth. He shuffled his feet, and the

sound echoed in the tiled hallway.

"Fiona?" he asked. "I know I didn't call first, but I didn't think you'd mind my dropping in. I have something for Devlin."

Cold quiet.

"Fiona?"

"What?"

"May I come in?"

The doorknob rattled.

Michael exhaled, stepped back, and lifted his head in anticipation of her opening the door.

Nothing happened.

With their differing schedules, Michael had not seen Fiona since earlier in the week when she and Cameron had gone off to lunch while he minded the store. Could Cameron have said something? No, his old friend would have voiced his suspicions in the open, with Michael right there to face them.

Then what was wrong? When he'd last seen Fiona, after pocketing the two coins, everything had been fine. Fiona had seemed weary, yes, and not particularly chatty, but nothing to indicate this cold reception.

"Fiona? What's the matter?" He rapped on the door lightly with one knuckle.

He heard her moving.

"Is something wrong?"

"Wrong?" She swung open the door. "You have the gall to come to my home after what you've done and ask me if anything is *wrong?*"

The gust of air fanned her hair from her face. She wore no makeup and stood before him barefoot, in jeans and a short-sleeved shirt.

The sight of her, even in a state of obvious displeasure,

made Michael smile. He leaned one shoulder against the door frame and cocked his head. "Well, good day to you, too, darlin' girl."

"Don't you 'darlin' girl' me, you—you…" She gripped the door with her right hand until her knuckles went white. "Well, I don't know what you are—or *who* you are, for that matter, Michael Shaughnessy."

"You've answered your own question. I'm Michael—the same man I was when last I saw you, the same man I was when I put that ring on your finger the other night." He motioned to the Claddagh ring.

Her gaze fixed on the spot where he pointed, her face contorted with disgust as though she had just now discovered herself wearing the piece.

"Not the way I see it, Michael." She held her hand up, fingers splayed, the design of the Claddagh turned toward him. Her green eyes flashed fire, but her voice rushed out with an icy calm. "The way I see it, you're the same man who gave me cause to remove this ring fifteen years ago, with the same heart, the same motives."

She grabbed at the ring and began to tug.

Michael stopped her, one hand enveloping both of hers. He kept his voice low in hopes it would not waver with the power of his emotions. "No, Fiona. That's not true."

"Your actions say otherwise."

"What actions?" He curved his hand into a caress of her fingers. "I don't know what you're talking about."

Her eyes accused him before her words could. Her hands trembled beneath his touch, and when she spoke, it was barely a rasping whisper. "You took those coins."

"Is that what this is about?"

Relief eased like warm liquid seeping through his bones. A

slow, rumbling laugh worked up from the pit of his stomach.

"It's not funny, Michael. It's not one bit funny."

"No, of course not, it's just that...well, there's been some-thing of a misunderstanding, that's all."

"Misunderstanding?" She showed no sign of believing him.

"Yes, and it's just the kind of thing that would happen to me, too, to have done one thing with the best of intentions, only to have it achieve just the opposite effect." He stepped forward.

Fiona stood her ground at the threshold.

He took her by the shoulders but did not try to move her aside. "Let me in, Fiona, and give me one minute. What I have to give Devin, I think, will give you a different opinion of me."

"Devin isn't here." She did not budge. "He had to go to an evening orientation session for summer school. Maybe you should come another time."

"Another time?" He didn't like the idea, but then he'd brought his gift for Devin, and if he wasn't here, perhaps he'd best wait. "When might be better?"

"Oh, I don't know." She pulled her shoulders away from his grasp. "Maybe one day in July—perhaps when it snows."

She started to shut the door.

Michael saw all his good intentions vanishing. He'd come to give this very special gift to Devin. However, if he held any hope of smoothing things over with Fiona, he had to do something fast.

Fiona looked away, still pushing at the door.

Now or never, Michael thought. He reached into his pocket. "Fiona, wait. Please."

"I'm sorry, Michael. You made your choice; now I'm making mine."

"But you've got it all wrong. And I can prove it to you."

111

As the front door began to swing toward him, he pulled the box open with a sharp creak and thrust it blindly into the closing gap.

Eight

"O h, Michael." Tears washed over Fiona's line of vision, yet she could still make out the beautiful handmade cross in the box in Michael's hand.

He pushed at the door to let himself in, and she did not resist. When he volunteered the open jewelry box, she accepted it to take a closer look at the piece.

The coins, now cut in half and hammered thin but with the markings still visible, were fashioned in a rough-looking but dazzling cross. If the half circles had not been elongated, it might have resembled a child's pinwheel, but as it was, the shape was beautifully unique. It hung on a fine gold chain and was about the same size as the ones Cameron and Michael wore, but its design left no doubt that it was wholly original.

While Fiona was staring at the cross, the rest of her senses pricked up, highly sensitive to Michael's presence. The door fell shut, and Michael's heavy footsteps followed the padding of her bare feet into the living room. She felt the warmth of his body on her back and smelled the mix of the shop's musty odors and crisp citrus aftershave on his skin.

She could also taste the bittersweet tang of crow as she took back all her harsh opinions of him. She turned and said softly, "That's why you wanted both my coin and yours, then? To make this?"

He took the box back, snapping it shut with a resounding clap before tucking it away.

"What else would you think?" The teasing gentleness in his

eyes told her he knew exactly what she had thought and in that very instant also conveyed that he did not blame her in the least for her misgivings.

"I—I thought…that is, I recalled…" She stepped near to him, her head upturned. "Oh, Michael, I couldn't help but remember the time you told me that if you had but one of those coins you could prove all your family's claims. Then when you said you wanted the coins for yourself, I assumed—"

"You assumed what anyone would, given my obsession with the gold and my past misdeeds." He put his hand to her cheek.

"I should have let you explain yourself." She pressed her palm to his chest.

"I've done nothing to deserve your showing that kind of confidence in me."

"Nothing?" She slapped at his arm. "You were my lifeline when Neal died, Michael. And since you've been back in our lives, you've worked hard and gone out of your way for both Devin and me."

He feigned modesty, his eyes shining with impish pride all the while.

"I have to tell you something, Michael." She couldn't help smiling back at him.

He lowered his head. "What?" His eyes grew dark, his touch gentle.

Suddenly, all the years, disappointments, and heartache fell away. Standing in the circle of his arms, she felt eighteen again and he, the only man she thought she could ever love. The memory swept away the present and sent the heat of a flush up her neck and over her face.

Michael tipped his head to the right. He wet his lips. "Fiona?"

Her mouth was open, she realized, a tiny gasp catching in her chest. "What?"

"You said you had to tell me something."

"Oh." She blinked. "Um, that is, yes. I just wanted to say that, except for these last few days, I couldn't help but think of how much you've put me in mind of the old days—of the young man I knew and cared for so long ago."

He arched one eyebrow. His gaze dipped to brush her parted lips. "Is that so?"

Her head inclined to one side. "That's so."

"And what do you propose we do about that, darlin' girl?"

"Do?" she asked, putting her lips in the perfect position for kissing.

And Michael took advantage of it.

The kiss took her neither by surprise nor by storm. Achingly sweet, Michael's embrace and the feel of his lips on hers showed a restrained passion, as if to ask for her permission without words.

She kneaded her fingers into the hard muscle of his arms to let him know she would not push him away.

He took the sign and pulled her closer still until his warmth, his tender longing, the very essence of the gentle kiss enveloped her.

In that moment, she knew she was no innocent young girl and he no callow youth who took love as lightly as the quest for gold and adventure. Life and time had mellowed them both emotionally but had also honed them into people sure of their faith and of what they wanted from one another.

As Michael drew his mouth from hers, she saw in his eyes that he wanted her, but that he would do no more about it than a kiss to show his affection. She slid her hands down his strong arms and, despite the quivering in her knees, found a faint smile for him to say she felt the same.

Their relationship, Fiona knew, had now entered a new level, and she was grateful that Michael had found a way, with the cross made from the coins, to connect the past and present and to include her son. Once Devin had seen the gift, she thought, everything would be all right. The past would finally be laid to rest, and they could face the future together, God willing, as a family.

"Do not store up for yourselves treasures on earth, where moth and rust destroy, and where thieves break in and steal. But store up for yourselves treasures in heaven, where moth and rust do not destroy, and where thieves do not break in and steal. For where your treasure is, there your heart will be also." Devin glanced up from the card Michael had hand-printed with the verse, concluding, "Matthew 6:19–21."

"I thought it was appropriate, all things considered," Michael said.

Beside him on the couch, sitting noticeably closer than she had ever done before, Fiona fidgeted with the piping on a throw pillow.

Devin perched on the edge of the chair across from them. He kept the heels of his athletic shoes off the ground. He knotted his fingers together, the card between his legs jiggling as he bounced on the balls of his feet. He'd come home from the summer school orientation meeting in a typical teenage mood: uncertain, anxious, perhaps a little embarrassed at having to attend the special class, and he tried to cover his feelings with a thin air of indifferent cockiness. Now to have two authority figures in his life sit him down and hand him a Scripture to read...

Michael could appreciate the boy's nervous reaction. He gave Fiona a wink, then extended the closed box to Devin.

"What—" Devin reached out tentatively to accept the offering. "What is it?"

"Michael made it himself." Fiona beamed with pride.

Why he had ever chosen gold coins and the pursuit of an old family folktale over that smile, he'd never understand. His pulse picked up, seeing it again and knowing he was the cause. Michael placed his hand on her back, not wanting to presume too much or to reveal any change in their relationship to Devin too soon. Best to let Fiona handle that while he concentrated on reestablishing his ties to the boy.

This very special token, Michael thought as he watched the boy put on a show of disinterest for their benefit, would go a long way toward doing just that. The handmade cross tied together their shared past and their spiritual future while providing the kind of gift that might be given from a father to a son.

The hinge of the jewelry box gave a long, low creak.

Michael reigned in an overly enthusiastic grin, wanting to let the boy feel free to react honestly.

Devin pulled the box open, his head down.

Fiona gripped the sleeve of Michael's T-shirt.

The boy's brow creased with confusion. "Is this...are these what I think they are?"

"It's a cross," Fiona murmured.

"I know it's a cross." The words came out hard, sharp. His expression echoed the harshness.

"Michael made it himself." Fiona's tone rang with controlled parental warning. "'Tis his old craft—the design of jewelry and metalsmithing."

"Yeah, I *know* that."

His hand still on her back, Michael felt the quick intake of breath through Fiona's pink T-shirt. Her muscles tensed. She drew in another staunch breath, probably storing up to admonish her son.

Before she could speak, Michael shifted forward on the couch. He dipped his head to seek out eye contact when he supplied the unspoken word so clearly dangling at the end of Devin's statement. "But?"

The boy looked up. Something akin to pain and anger flashed in the boy's eyes. His jaw clenched, and a bright red color burst in the hollows of his freckled cheeks.

Never had he seen such animosity from this child, not even when he had kept the boy from his mother in order to secure the gold from Cameron. It hurt and dazed Michael. And as he swept his gaze from Devin's rage-filled scowl to the cross and back again, he asked himself how his good deed could have gone so strangely awry.

"What is it, Devin?" he asked. He squared his shoulders, trying to be a solid role model for the boy while at the same time not giving in to some adolescent fit of ingratitude.

Fiona scooted forward until she almost slid off the couch. "I'll tell you what it is—"

"No, Fiona." Michael put his hand out, straight-armed as though restraining her physically. "I think this is between the two of us."

Devin's mouth twitched.

"Am I right, son?"

"Don't call me son." The boy's voice was a low growl.

"I thought so." He forced himself to relax his posture. Slowly, he put one ankle up on the opposite knee, draped an arm over his raised leg, and cocked the other arm over the back of the couch.

Devin watched. He stopped his legs from jiggling and braced his forearms on his knees, the box tipped outward so that the cross hung at an odd angle.

"It's obvious there's something you want to say to me, Devin." Michael lifted his chin. "What is it? Don't you like your gift?"

The boy's right leg began to shake again. Still, he kept his low voice steady when he burned his gaze into Michael's and said, "These are some of the coins."

"Yes, they are."

"I recognize them from when Uncle Cam and I found the buried treasure."

"I thought you might." Michael nodded.

Devin twisted the box and studied its contents, his mouth set in a grim line. "How did you get these?"

"Your Uncle Cam brought them to us," Fiona said. "He got them as a reward for the gold having been returned to its rightful owners and—"

"Rightful owners?" Devin shot up from his seat to tower over the both of them. "We are the rightful owners!"

Michael stood up. He anchored his feet wide to keep Fiona from standing too, in an instinctively protective gesture.

"You don't know what you're saying, Devin," he said calmly.

"Oh, don't I?" He leaned forward, his narrow chest puffed out. "I know that with just one o' these coins, the only heir to the Shaughnessy half o' the fortune could prove what the rest o' us Shaughnessys and O'Deas have known for a hundred years—that the gold was not stolen. It was *ours*."

As Devin spoke, his words thickened with the old brogue, which for Michael added a power and passion he had not expected. Still, he tried to mollify the boy. "Sit back down and let us talk this through reasonably."

"Talk what through? Your trying to change my mind as yours has been, or your complete betrayal of both our families by doing *this* to the gold pieces that could have vindicated us all?"

Devin threw the box at Michael with such vehemence that one corner jabbed his chest. The box struck his knee, snapped shut like a bullet hitting its mark, then tumbled to the floor.

If the gift had been anything else at all, Michael would have simply dealt with the boy's bratty behavior with a firm but patient hand. But this—to throw down the cross, the handmade gift of the coins that he had come so far to be able to part with himself—was nothing short of a total rejection of everything Michael held dear.

"Devin O'Dea, you apologize to your Uncle Mike this instant." Fiona pressed against Michael as she forced her way past the shield he provided with his body. "What has gotten into you?"

Michael bent down to scoop up the discarded gift at his feet.

"Me?" Devin stabbed one finger in accusation at Michael. "Why don't you ask Uncle Mike what's gotten into *him*?"

Michael pressed his fingertips against the tiny hinges on the blue box. He froze, still bent over, and raised his head, his eyes narrowed. "The truth, son—that's what's gotten into me. The truth about our family legacy and the truth about myself as well."

"The truth? How can you know the truth unless you use a coin to unveil it?"

"The truth is not in any coin, Devin." Michael clicked the box open and held it up to confront Devin with its contents. "This is the truth—the only treasure that matters. Not redemption of some misconceived concept of honor, but salvation of the soul."

"You just don't get it." The boy gestured broadly, turning on his heel to walk away, then turning again to face Fiona and Michael. "If you put that gold ahead of your beliefs, then that's your problem, not mine. *I* can have my faith and my honor, as my father sought to have before me."

Michael turned to Fiona. "Neal…?"

She nodded to let him know that her late husband, unlike his brother, Cameron, had believed that the gold was his birthright.

"Why did you think I did what I did?" Devin pushed both his hands back through his hair, his face flushed. "I could have just told you that Uncle Cam and I had found the gold or told the social worker who handed me over to you who you were and ended it all there and then. But I remembered the stories Dad told me, that with one coin, the Shaughnessys and the O'Deas could reclaim their rightful property."

Michael had assumed that Devin kept quiet about finding the gold because he believed as Cameron did that it was ill-gotten gain and should be returned. He thought the boy had not identified him to Julia, the social worker who had inadvertently gotten involved, out of loyalty to Cameron. It never occurred to him that Devin had been playing some kind of game.

"Both ends against the middle," Michael muttered, his mind still trying to form a clear picture of what had happened.

"What?" Fiona asked.

"That's what you were doing, isn't it?" He shook his head in wonder that he hadn't realized it before. "You didn't tell anyone the whole truth so that there would still be a chance that I would get to the gold first or perhaps extort it from your Uncle Cam in exchange for your safe return."

The boy would not meet his eyes.

"Then you got Julia, who just happened to find you baby-sitting the gold, suckered into the mess by having her dig up

121

the treasure. What was your hope there, Devin? That having her take responsibility for the gold would stall your Uncle Cam from getting it?"

"Uncle Cam's heart was in the right place, I'm sure. But when it came to matters of the gold and the family, his head was in the clouds."

"That's your father talking, Devin," Fiona said, almost as if to herself rather than as an admonishment.

The boy stuffed his hands in his pockets, his shoulders hunched. His green eyes narrowed to slits, and a lock of red hair fell over his forehead. "That's my heritage talking. And now that's gone forever—thanks to *him*."

"Devin, that's not..." Fiona's words fell away.

Devin spun on his heel and strode from the room, carried by his own anger.

Fiona opened her mouth to call to him, but the window-rattling *wham* of his bedroom door slamming cut her off.

She heaved a heavy sigh and pressed her fingertips to the faint furrow between her eyebrows. Her head hurt with the churning possibilities of what she should do next.

Michael maneuvered past the coffee table to reach Fiona. Standing behind her, he cupped his hands over her slumped shoulders and pulled her back so that her rigid spine rested against his chest.

His touch made her relax.

He leaned down. "Why didn't you tell me?"

"About Neal and his believing as you did about the gold?"

Michael nodded.

"Why would I tell you that?" Her eyes widened, but that did not stop the bath of unshed tears that softened her view of Michael's concerned face. She swallowed hard and whispered, "It would have only fueled your cause. Enough damage was done already without that."

"You're right. If I had known when I came back into your life after Neal's death that he had shared my views, I'd have felt more justified in my obsession than before." He slid his hand down one of her arms, then up again.

She fought the urge to shiver.

"I might have taken it further, perhaps done whatever it took to keep Cameron from taking that gold back to Ireland."

"I thought as much. And once you'd changed in your heart toward the gold, there seemed no need to tell you how Neal felt about it." She took his hand and laid the back of it against her cheek. "Perhaps now you understand why I want to shelter Devin from even a single coin until he's older."

"It's a wise decision."

"That gold is a curse." She turned to lean her shoulder against his broad chest.

"A curse?" He cocked an eyebrow to give her the hint of a grin. "'Tis a wee bit of the fanciful Irish coming out in you now, isn't it, lass?"

She shut her eyes and gave a quick laugh. "All right, I don't really believe it is cursed, but I do know this—no good has ever come from that stolen gold or the quest to get it back. It has stripped everyone involved with it of something they held dear."

"That's true enough." He tipped her chin up with one finger. "It cost my grandfather his freedom—the very thing he'd wanted to gain by taking the gold so that he could emigrate to America."

"It cost Grandfather O'Dea the same."

"It took my father's will to work." Michael's mouth set in a hard scowl as it often did when the talk turned to his father. "It took his hope and his ability to care about the people he said he wanted the treasure to build a better life for—his family."

She laid her hand over his heart, hoping to give him some solace. "It took my father-in-law's honor. It made him a hollow man with little allegiance to anything but a legend."

He stroked her chin with his thumb. "And from Cameron and me it took much of our youth—the years growing up under its shadow as well as the years when we might have done more with our lives, including having families."

She thought for an instant of the life that might have been with Michael but quickly put that aside to think of what had been instead—her life with Neal.

She cast her gaze downward. "It created a hardness in Neal that affected our marriage and, worst of all, his relationship with Devin."

"That's why the boy feels doubly betrayed."

"Yes." The word broke in a harsh whisper. A lone tear rolled down Fiona's cheek, but she made no move to brush it away. "He not only feels the sting of losing what he's been taught is his family's due, but he must feel as though he has played a hand in losing the one thing his father cared most about."

Michael said nothing for a moment. He just stood there, his hand curved around her cheek.

Fiona felt her heart beat harder as she anticipated what was to come. She knew without hearing it what Michael must be thinking, yet she felt helpless to stop him from saying it aloud and forcing her to confront a painful reality.

Finally, his eyes grim, he wet his lips and spoke. "There's still one coin left, Fiona."

She bit her lip.

"That's all it would take—"

"No!" She pushed away from him. "Please. Don't even suggest it."

He caught her by the wrist before she could turn.

"I'm not saying it for my own sake, Fiona. If you like, I'll give you everything you need to handle it completely on your own. I'll bow out entirely."

She blinked, suddenly aware of the hot tears flooding her eyes. "You'd...you'd do that? Give me the ability to prove the right or wrong of the driving force in your life these many years?"

"I would and I will." He curved his fingers into her palm. "Just say the word, Fiona."

"Why, Michael?" Her throat strangled on the question, but she had to ask. She had to hear his motivation from his own mouth. "Why would you do that?"

"Here's why." He took up the blue box again and flipped it open with one hand to expose the cross crafted of gold coins. "Because I know where my treasure is now, Fiona. I'd lost sight of it. Like Devin, I thought my goals and my greed created no conflict with my faith. Now I see otherwise."

She looked from the glittering cross to the new light shining in Michael's eyes.

"You can't force Devin to change his mind by denying him the gold. That will only serve to build it up in his mind to something far more powerful than most any man could handle."

He released her wrist and clamped the box shut.

Her hand fell like lead to her side.

"Think about it, Fiona." He stepped away from her, tucking the box in his pocket. "Whenever you're ready to make that decision, my offer will stand ready."

N i n e

"D evin?" Fiona knocked lightly on the hollow wooden door. "Devin, answer me. I mean it."

From inside the room, bedsprings creaked, the floor squeaked, footsteps shuffled, then the doorknob cranked slowly to the left.

"Is *he* still here?" One half-shut eye peered at her from the two-inch crack between the door and the frame.

"No."

What she could see of his lower lip was pushed out in a pout.

She folded her arms over her chest and positioned her feet to stand her ground.

The doorknob rattled.

Fiona cocked her head to issue a warning.

Devin groaned and swung the door inward.

"That's more like it, young man."

"Well, as long as *he's* gone, I guess I can leave the door open." The boy lumbered over to his bed as if the act were almost more than he could manage.

Where was the delightful little boy who used to run into her arms for a hug or who would dash off to bed ahead of her so he could be waiting to say his prayers, a storybook already tucked beneath the covers?

She glanced from the laundry hamper, with limp socks scattered like confetti around it, to the poster of a sports car thumbtacked to the closet door. The gooseneck desk lamp threw long shadows around the room, which seemed to make the stack of school books and papers on the desk multiply. Fiona moved her son's slouching backpack from the desk chair and plunked herself down.

Devin threw himself into a heap on the bed, the mattress compressing beneath him. He rolled onto his side and bunched the pillow beneath his cheek, then finally looked at her.

In his oversized T-shirt and baggy denim shorts, his hair a rumpled mess, Fiona decided he still did resemble that boy she'd nearly surrendered to teenage angst and confusion. Adding to that impression was the fact that he wore an expression so forlorn he looked like a little boy who'd lost his friend.

Fiona blinked. She sat up in the chair, her attention focused on her son through casual side glances.

Devin had lost his father and his grandfather. Then he'd felt betrayed by his Uncle Cam's returning the gold. Now he thought he'd been let down by his last male role model, the man who had acted more like a father to him than his own flesh-and-blood parent had. That must scare him more than he wanted anyone to know.

Devin did not want to lose Michael.

Despite her son's horrid behavior earlier, Fiona suddenly felt hopeful. With enough time and patience, she and Michael could mend this rift and put things back on a level footing again. She just had to find a way to throw the two of them together again, to give them another common goal to work toward together.

Her teeth sank into her lower lip as she scanned the surroundings for some excuse to unite the two. Almost immediately, her gaze fell on a crumpled paper folded in quarters on Devin's cluttered desk.

The summer-school guidelines. That was it.

"Listen, son, I know you're feeling hurt and disappointed right now." She swiveled to the left, stopped herself, then swiveled back again, hard pressed to contain her exuberance for her idea. "But you'll be getting over that soon enough, I'm thinking."

"No, I won't." He punched his pillow, then stuck his chin into the plump center.

"Oh, sweetheart, yes, you will. Pretty soon you and your Uncle Mike—"

"He's not my uncle."

"No, not technically. But he is your godfather, and he cares about you like a blood uncle would." She laced one arm around her ribcage and lightly rested the other on top of it. How much, she wondered, could she intimate about her budding feelings for Michael without upsetting Devin even more?

In the silence she could hear the boy's teeth grind together, his whole face red from trying to cope with the landslide of emotion this evening's events had unleashed.

Best not to push it, she decided.

"Your Uncle Mike loves you, son. And he deserves better than this from you."

"He *deserves?*" Devin sat up and the pillow plopped onto the floor. "Mom, he didn't just let me down, he let down our whole family. He let down Dad."

A tremor passed through his body. His usually ruddy face went pale, and tears formed along the rims of his eyes.

The sight tore at Fiona's heart. Still, as a mother, she knew she must do what was best for her child, not what humored him or what made him feel temporarily better. She drew her shoulders up and went to him, settling beside him on the bed.

"Devin, darlin', no one let your father down." She put one

arm around his shoulders, nuzzling his hair with the tip of her nose. "Not Michael, not me, and especially not you."

"Me?" he rasped. "I never said *I* let him down. I never said that."

"Maybe you didn't have to."

He blinked. He sniffled. He shuddered out a shaky breath. He hung his head.

"Oh, sweetheart." She moved to kneel in front of him and placed her face beneath her son's.

He gulped back a sob.

"Your father had his own ideas, but they were just that—*his* ideas. You're not responsible for seeing that those notions get carried on or carried out." She placed her hand along his cheek. "Do you understand that?"

Devin nodded.

"And you can't hold your Uncle Mike responsible for that, either."

His jaw clenched. "He had no right to do what he did with those coins."

"He had every right—and what's more, he had every reason."

Devin looked away.

"Just as I have my own reasons for—" She stopped herself. She had not wanted to tell Devin of the coin Cameron left for him, but seeing the pain in her child's eyes, she knew she could not keep it from him. Knowing that one coin still existed, that it would be waiting for him when he was mature enough to deal with it, might soften him toward both Cameron and Michael.

"Devin, there's something very important I need to tell you, but I want you to promise to listen to me, not to argue or whine or throw some manner of temper fit."

"Mom." He rolled his eyes at the suggestion of such childish behavior.

"Promise," she demanded.

He wrinkled up his nose. "Mom, I'm too old for that."

"Promise, or I won't be telling you a thing."

He groaned.

She did not need an interpreter to tell her that the long, plaintive sound meant he thought she was hopelessly out of touch and what Americans called 'corny.'

Finally, he met her gaze. "Okay, I promise."

"I'm glad you've decided to handle this like a grown-up, son, because I know you are not going to like what I have to tell you." A knot formed in her chest, but she forced the words past it. "There is a third gold piece."

"A third?" He made a face halfway between a grin and a sneeze. "There's a third coin? One that hasn't been cut up?"

She nodded. "The reward was one coin for each of the surviving members of the O'Dea and Shaughnessy families."

"Whose is it?"

She rubbed her palm over the textured fabric of his bedspread. Suddenly she wished she'd never brought up the subject. The eagerness shining in her son's eyes reminded her too much of the look Neal used to get when he spoke of getting his hands on the gold. It frightened her.

She swallowed hard and thought how easy it would be to claim the remaining coin belonged to her, or even to Michael. The cross had been a gift for Devin, after all. It was no stretch of the imagination to think that one of the coins used had been his.

"Mom? Who does the other coin belong to?"

She blinked to keep from tearing up as she stroked her son's cheek with one hand. "You. The coin belongs to you, Devin."

"Yes!" He pushed up from the bed with more energy than she'd seen him display in months. "Where is it? Can I see it now?"

"It's not at the house. I thought it best to keep it locked up. It's in the safe at the shop."

"But I can see it someday, right?"

"Well, someday, yes, when you're—"

Devin nabbed her by the shoulders and cut her off, his face aglow. "Do you know what this means, Mom? This changes everything!"

"This changes nothing." She stood. "At least for the time being."

"What do you mean? With that one coin we can prove— that is, Uncle Mike can prove—" He jerked his head up, his eyes narrowed to angry slits. "That's it, isn't it? Even if I have the coin, Uncle Mike won't help me use it to prove anything, will he?"

"Not without my permission he won't."

"I knew it. I knew he'd stand between us and—"

"Michael is only doing what's best for you, as am I."

"It's not fair, Mom. It's not."

"No, it doesn't seem that way." She patted him on the back. "But there'll come a day when you'll appreciate what your uncle tried to do for you today."

"I doubt it," he mumbled.

"And you'll thank him for his concern."

He looked up at her, his head still lowered. "To thank him I'd have to speak to him, and I don't see much chance of that happening anytime soon."

"Oh, you don't, do you?" She plunked her fists on her hips.

"No, ma'am, I don't."

"Then I'll wager you're in for a long, quiet summer, lad."

He jerked his head up. "Why?"

"Because whether or not you're speaking to him, he'll be speaking to you, because—"

"Yeah, yeah, because he loves me."

"Not just that, young man." She strolled to the door. Then, placing her hand on the door frame, she spun around to deliver her punch line. "Your Uncle Mike will be talking a great deal to you this summer, because whether you like it or not—he's going to be your tutor."

She walked away feeling mighty pleased with herself until she heard Devin's final comment called after her in the darkened hallway.

"I may have to tolerate him in order to pass my math course, but no one can make me like it. And no one on this earth can *ever* make me forgive him for what he's done."

"I'll be right there, Mr. Gadberry." Michael tightened the last bracket on the security camera he was mounting over the shop door.

Gadberry had decided that the system, consisting of two tiny cameras that fed a continuous view of the shop into small black-and-white monitors in his upstairs apartment, provided the perfect solution. Michael had argued that it seemed an extravagance, given that the shop had never experienced anything but a few petty shoplifting incidents. Gadberry, however, had wanted the system, and he was the boss.

That one interaction with the man had given Michael a new appreciation for all Fiona had endured working here these last few years. It had also made him more determined than ever to help her find a way around the eccentric and headstrong Gadberry to better her work situation.

Still atop the ladder, he pointed with the screwdriver to an out-of-the-way spot Fiona had cleared for Gadberry's latest find. "Fiona and I thought that might show better over there."

"There? Who'll see it there?" The older man sniffed.

Michael climbed down the ladder and closed it with a good deal of metallic clanging, then leaned it against the wall so he could offer Gadberry a hand.

Gadberry refused the outstretched arms with a wobble of his head. "No, Michael my boy, there is only one place good enough for *this* little treasure."

"The Dumpster?" Michael asked under his breath as Fiona passed with two chatty customers.

Fiona chuckled.

Gadberry stumbled to the left, huffed out a breath, then overcorrected to the right with the burden he refused to allow Michael to help him carry. "This is an authentic piece, circa 1967. They used to sell them in the same stores with plastic beaded curtains, lava lamps, and beanbag chairs. Remember those?"

"Actually, I was still in Ireland then, sir, but I've seen bean-bag chairs and lava lamps since I've been in America."

"Reproductions." Gadberry dragged the word out with obvious distaste. "It's this retro craze. But this." He clunked the heavy object down in an open space in the front window, then stepped back to admire it. "This is the original goods. You can tell by the use of lead-based paint and the fact that it's all one piece, not separately manufactured parts all glued together."

"I'm sure that's part of its charm, sir."

"Look at it, Shaughnessy." The man's broad smile shone almost as brightly as the sweat glistening on his forehead. "It took me a long time to find this. Now tell me honestly, have you ever seen anything like it?"

"No, sir, I can honestly say I haven't." Michael shook his head, reaching out to pat the backside of the shimmering plaster elephant, whose trunk was raised to provide a socket for a lightbulb. The movement knocked the gold-toned lamp shade askew, setting its sombrero ball fringe to swinging. "Never seen anything like that before in my entire life."

"Collectibles, son." Gadberry tipped his head and winked an eye. "That's where the money's at. Collectibles."

"You're saying someone would want to start a collection of these things?" Michael straightened the lamp shade. The fringe bobbed again.

Fiona grinned as she led the ladies past to show them something in the display case behind Michael.

"Well, no, not a whole collection. Perhaps a pair, though." Gadberry stood back, his arms folded over his rounded chest. "Wouldn't a pair of those be something?"

"Oh, they'd be something all right." Michael twisted his head to whisper to Fiona, "Something to give your children nightmares."

Fiona cleared her throat to disguise a giggle. "These, ladies, are the goblets I was telling you about. Handcrafted in Ireland in a town not far from the very village where I grew up."

The two women oohed and ahhed and stepped up to the case, their heads together as they murmured their opinions to one another.

"And why is it they didn't come from our very own village, Mrs. O'Dea?" Michael craned his neck to study the simple but elegant goblets in the case. "We've got the craftsmen, and heaven knows, they need the work."

The women fell silent, their heads lifted to observe the exchange.

Fiona's face froze in an unnatural smile. "Yes, well, all of

Ireland is dotted with every kind of craftsman imaginable, isn't it? And many who could use the work, as well."

"Yes, but if you're going to the trouble of importing glass from all that way, why not go a wee bit further and help the economy of friends and family in a town you know and love?" He tilted his head back in hopes of making his argument heard by Gadberry. He could see in Fiona's eyes that she did not yet suspect he had a plan in pursuing this line of questioning. "It's a simple enough thing to make the contacts and do your buying from—"

"I don't do the buying, Mr. Shaughnessy." She said his name, but her gaze fixed on Gadberry's back as the other man leaned over to situate the 'collectible' just so in the window.

The women, still facing the counter in pretense of admiring the goblets, pricked up their ears like hunting dogs waiting for the chase.

Michael tried not to grin and give away his intentions.

"If you have an idea for what we should import in the future, perhaps you can take it up with the owner," she said at full volume, her pointed gaze enough to penetrate almost anything but Gadberry's thick hide. She rolled her eyes skyward, her jaw still clenched in a phony smile when she muttered, "For all the good it will do you."

"Take what up with the owner?" Gadberry turned carefully, encumbered by his weight and his stooped position.

"About acquiring goods for the shop, sir." Michael folded his arms.

"I handle all the acquisitions personally."

"And what a fine job you do, too, sir." From the corners of his eyes, Michael saw Fiona tense. He slapped Gadberry lightly on the back and motioned toward the man's latest addition. "I wouldn't dare to tell you a thing about the…um, collectibles market, but I would like to make a recommendation about some of the imported goods."

Michael stole a glance at Fiona. The incident between Devin and him had put a strain on his blossoming relationship with her. Though the boy had agreed to allow Michael's tutoring and would be in this evening for his first session, an awkwardness still hung between Fiona and him.

Michael sensed that they were not on the same side anymore, even if they shared the same goals, faith, and feelings. What he was about to do could change that. For once he had an opportunity to shine the light on Fiona, to help her get what she so wanted at work: Gadberry's respect and the chance to implement her ideas to improve the shop.

"Well, if you've got something to say, Shaughnessy, say it," Gadberry urged.

"I was just thinking, Mr. Gadberry. That is, after listening to Mrs. O'Dea, it occurred to me...."

"What is it?"

"Well, while your taste and selection in antiques is impeccable..." Michael said, and it was no lie. If the man had chosen to sell only antiques, Fiona's input would hardly be needed. "And while you have a certain..."

Gadberry eyed him.

Choose your words carefully, Michael warned himself. Threatening the ego of a man like Gadberry would do Fiona more harm than good. He cocked his head, gave what he hoped would pass for a thoughtful expression, and waved his hand with a casual flourish. "Let's say, a *flair* for buying the odd knickknack and...um, compelling decorative pieces—"

Gadberry frowned, his chin pushed up and his lip out so that he looked like a bulldog sucking a sour lemon. "Just what is it you're getting at?"

"He just means, sir, that a wise man uses his resources, um—" Fiona wet her lips, then brightened up. "Wisely."

Michael nodded. She was on to his scheme and was willing to play along. "That's right, sir," he said. "And a wise businessman knows how to delegate—"

"Wisely," Fiona finished.

"You know what I think, Shaughnessy?" Gadberry stuck out his chest. "I think there's only one of us around here that's wise and it's you. You're a wise—"

"Ah, spare me your compliments, Mr. Gadberry." Michael held up his hand and turned his head in feigned modesty. "At least until you've heard me out and have every reason to praise my wisdom."

The two women customers, who had been enthralled by the goings-on, laughed aloud.

Fiona smiled weakly.

Gadberry harrumphed.

"How would you describe your shop?" Michael asked. "That is, if someone were to ask what it is you sell at Gadabout Gifts, how would you answer them?"

Gadberry lifted both his chins and recited the words from the company letterhead. "Unique gifts, antiques, and collectibles from around the world. Something to appeal to everyone on your shopping list."

Michael gave Fiona a we've-got-him-now wink, then placed his hand on Gadberry's shoulder. "Ah, your premise is, then, that you carry a variety of items meant to appeal to the broad spectrum of shoppers."

"It is."

"And you alone do the ordering and buying for the shop?"

"I see where you're heading with this, Shaughnessy." He scowled.

"If I may, sir," Fiona said, wearing a demeanor of polite ambition. "It does make sense to me that, in order to have the broadest appeal, one should rely on more than one person's taste."

Gadberry's bushy brows angled down. "What's wrong with my taste?"

"Nothing," Michael said quickly. "Nothing at all."

Fiona gave the elephant lamp a squint-eyed glare, which she then turned on Michael.

He responded with a grin. "However, I wonder if perhaps you're spreading yourself a bit too thin."

"How's that?"

"Well, let's take, for example, our little friend here." Michael patted the elephant. "With the lead paint and no glue."

"What about it?"

"What about it is that I would never have known an authentic…um, elephant lamp from a reproduction."

"Cheap knockoffs," Gadberry grumbled.

"But you wouldn't make that mistake because you've taken time learning the business, making trustworthy contacts, and looking for only the best pieces."

"At the best prices," Gadberry added.

"Anything less would be unthinkable." Michael gave a dismissive wave, then let his hand fall on Fiona's shoulder.

"You never told me, Michael Shaughnessy," she whispered with Michael's body a shield between her and her boss.

"Told you what?" he replied in kind, aware that Gadberry could not hear, but the wide-eyed lady customers could.

"That those lips which so sweetly kissed my own had also kissed the Blarney stone."

"Good one," one of the woman called out.

"What was that?" Gadberry edged in behind Michael.

He turned. "The lady was just saying what a good point I made."

"I wasn't aware you had made a point."

"Well, then, let me make it again for you, sir." He gave a magnanimous wave of his hand. "My point is that it takes time to acquire the right pieces for a unique shop such as Gadabout Gifts."

"That's the most sensible thing you've said in this whole conversation, son."

"But time spent on one thing—say, finding authentic collectibles—means time taken away from something else, such as Irish glassware."

Gadberry snorted. "Glassware is glassware. You open a catalog and point to some. Problem solved."

"Oh, but you're wrong, sir." Fiona hurried around the display case, unlocked its hinged back, and slipped one goblet from the shelf. "Ireland has a long history of glass-making, and many towns have their own studios, each producing its own individualized product."

"Is that so?"

"That's so," Michael assured him. "Our countrymen are famous for the unique nature of their goods. Take, for example, an Irish fisherman's sweater."

"Oh, yes." Fiona held up her hand, jumping in to show off her expertise just as Michael hoped she would. "Did you know those intricate patterns in the design of those lovely hand-knit sweaters are a message?"

"A message?" one of the ladies asked.

By his expression, Gadberry showed piqued interest, but he did not voice it.

"Why, yes." Fiona spread her hands to gesture as she spoke in a lilting whisper. "While the sea provided feast and fortune, it also took many a brave lad under, his spirit gone on to glory but his body lost among the waves."

Gadberry inched closer.

"So it was that the women of the small coastal villages fashioned sweaters for their men, each town having its own unique design. By the design of the ribbing, the twists and turns, braids and ridges, they found a way of telling someone who found a sailor's body washed up upon the shore where to send him home for burial." Fiona intertwined her fingers in illustration. "And so in Ireland a sweater is not just a sweater, it also says something about who you are and where—"

"That's an Irish piece, too, isn't it?" The older of the two ladies snatched at Fiona's hand.

Michael tensed. "That's a Claddagh ring. Irish, yes, but we don't handle jewelry here and so—"

"You don't?" The second woman lowered her head over the ring to inspect it before lifting her gaze to Fiona's face. "So tell me then, where did you get it? It's lovely."

"Thank you." She cast a sly sidelong look at Michael.

He parted his lips to steer the conversation back to Fiona's knowledge and ability, but she slipped her hand from the woman's grasp and thrust it toward Gadberry.

"It is lovely, isn't it, Mr. Gadberry?"

"Well, yes, it is quite—"

"Michael made it."

"Made?" Gadberry frowned.

"Michael? You mean this fellow here?" The older woman tugged at Michael's shirt sleeve. "You *made* that?"

"Most artists of Michael's caliber use the term *designed*," Fiona said.

He would have cut the conversation off right there. But after all they had been through lately, to hear the level of pride in

Fiona's voice reserved just for him, well, it did Michael's heart too much good.

"Do you have a catalog of your work?" The older woman asked, shaking his sleeve to command attention. "Or can I commission a similar piece from you?"

He'd meant to put the focus on Fiona, to give her a shot at that promotion and the buying position she longed for. "I don't do that kind of thing any—"

"He just designed a breathtaking piece for my son." Fiona turned to Gadberry. "It's just the kind of thing our clientele would adore."

That got the old man's attention more than anything else said so far. "Any chance that I could see this masterpiece, Shaughnessy?"

His jaw tightened as his gaze honed in on Fiona.

She did not take the hint. "Show him, Michael."

"I don't have it on me," he muttered.

"Well, he does have another example of his work on him." Fiona touched her fingertips to her throat. "Show them your cross, Michael."

"I…um…" He put his fist to his mouth and coughed. He had to find a way to get back to showcasing Fiona, not him or his work. "I'd rather—"

The shop door swung open, sending a glaring reflection across the floor and glass countertop, and making the goblets behind Fiona twinkle.

The mail carrier saluted them with a small packet of envelopes, then laid it on the counter as he always did, slipping back outside without a word.

Michael used the distraction to step up to the goblet case to direct the conversation away from him. "Besides, I thought you ladies were interested in glassware." He opened the case to

142

withdraw one fine goblet. "Just look at this piece."

"It's beautiful, to be sure, Michael, but—"

"I *have* always admired that style," one of the ladies interrupted Fiona.

Gadberry easily turned his focus on the object. After all, these were customers, and this was something he could sell them, unlike Michael's jewelry. "Sell a lot of that kind of thing, we do."

"Which means you have to *buy* a lot of them, true?" Michael said.

"True."

Michael relaxed. Now they were back on track. Fiona would have that raise in no time. He twirled the stem of the goblet between his fingers. "What if I told you, Mr. Gadberry, that you could get a piece just as lovely, if not more so, and for a better price?"

"I could?" Gadberry's tone registered doubt.

"I'd be interested," one of the ladies volunteered.

"Just as you know so much about antiques and collectibles, you have someone on staff who not only understands Irish crafts but also has the knowledge, the skill, and the contacts to bring them into your store with little or no involvement from you."

"Go on." He did not sound convinced, but he did not disregard the notion, either.

Michael drew a deep breath. "I'm just suggesting that you rethink the way you utilize your employees—and perhaps consider a promotion and pay raise for any added work, of course."

"Of course. Of course." Gadberry nodded as though it had all suddenly fallen into place.

After all the years working here, Michael thought, Fiona

was finally going to get what she deserved—and she had no one but Michael Shaughnessy to thank for it.

"I see what you're getting at, Shaughnessy, and not to worry." Gadberry reached out and slammed his meaty palm against Michael's back. "You've certainly convinced me. Consider yourself the new buyer for all our Irish imported goods. Congratulations."

T e n

How could this have happened? Fiona settled onto her couch with a spoon in one hand and a pint of ice cream in the other. One minute she'd been happily nudging Michael along toward a career crafting fine jewelry, just as he'd been helping her score points with Gadberry.

Then *wham!* Michael got her promotion.

Lord bless him, he had tried to decline it. She peeled up the lid to her comfort food of choice for the evening, her mind still whirring over the recent events. Michael had tried to explain to Mr. Gadberry that he'd meant for Fiona to become his Irish buyer, but to no avail.

So much for that, she thought. Nothing she could change now.

She sighed. The lid made a satisfying *plop* when she set it down on the coffee table. She dangled her spoon above the ice cream.

"It's not fair." She borrowed one of Devin's favorite expressions, stabbing the point of the spoon again and again into the vanilla with chocolate swirls. "It's just not fair."

Tears that had threatened to fall ever since Gadberry's announcement sprang up along her lashes. She turned her face heavenward. "I'm not bitter, Lord. Really, I'm not."

She let go of the spoon, leaving it protruding from the ice cream as she closed her eyes.

"I'm not angry or jealous, either—exactly. It's not Michael's fault, after all, that Gadberry is the way he is." She pressed her lips together for a moment, but the pause did not strengthen her. Her voice thinned and trembled as she went on. "It's just that, Lord, I've been so good—or at least I've tried to be. And Michael—"

She drew in a shuddering breath. Much as she had come to care for the man, she could not pretend, especially in prayer, that he was anything more than he honestly was. "Michael has been a mess. He's hurt people, Lord. He's hurt me. And yet, he always seems to be the one rewarded."

She hugged herself, her eyes closing tighter as the tears washed over her cheeks. "I don't begrudge Michael his good fortune, his blessings. Knowing him as I do, knowing the man he has become, I celebrate the good things that have come to him. I am grateful for them because they've helped to shape him into the good man he is today."

He *was* a good man, too. She knew it to the core of her being. He clearly regretted whatever wrongs he'd done in the past and looked to the future with the kind of hope that only comes to a man who knows he is forgiven—and loved. Loved by God, and, as long as she was using unvarnished honesty, she might as well admit it—loved by her as well.

Confessing the truth of it, even in silence in the safety of her quiet apartment, made Fiona uneasy. It sent a shiver over her skin despite the warmth it generated through her body. She'd fallen in love with a man who could, with the decision to prove the gold belonged to his family, break her heart—again.

Deep within her, anxiety stirred like slow poison in her veins. She'd worked so hard, played by all the rules, done what had been expected and then some. Why wasn't there more comfort and hope in *her* life?

"What about me, Lord?" The question lacked self-pity or

torment. "When will I, as Devin might say, 'get a break'? I'm so weary of waiting for it. If only I knew what your plan was—"

The plea pulled her up short, making her feel foolish for her indulgence. A slow smile worked across her lips. "But then, I suppose I *do* know, don't I? 'In all things God works for the good of those who love him.'"

She blew out the briefest of laughs. Her head still bent in prayer, she went on, "I've heard it said that the best way to get along with God is to stay out of his chair. I guess I'll do that now and trust that this will work out, because I do truly love you, Lord. Amen."

She lifted her chin, still feeling blue about losing the job but with a new sense of peace and goodwill. She scrubbed her lingering tears away with the back of her hand, then snatched up the spoon still protruding from the melting ice cream.

"Nothing to do now but drown my sorrows in a carton of fudge ripple," she murmured. She clicked the TV on to watch something totally mindless and enjoy some quiet time before she had to pick Devin up from tutoring at nine o'clock.

"I guess I should be thankful," she said, just as she raised a heaping spoonful of ice cream to her lips. "My biggest problem right now can be solved by my simple trust in God and something swimming in chocolate."

The jarring ring of the telephone, however, kept her from taking that bite.

Michael glanced at the large brass-and-marble mantel clock above his darkened fireplace. Competing for his attention on either side of the clock were the two small, black-and-white TV monitors standing out in glaring contrast to the subdued atmosphere of the antique furnishings. Their sizzling static, as they flickered with grainy views of the empty shop below, grated on his already sensitive nerves.

His attention fell on the clock again. Seven-thirty. Where was Devin?

According to Fiona, the boy had gone to a friend's house after his summer-school class let out. The friend's mother was going to take them out for a bite to eat, then drop Devin off at Michael's apartment. That should have happened thirty minutes ago.

Around the small apartment, the carefully selected furniture gleamed in the low glow of the overhead light. Michael leaned back on the cherry love seat, then sat forward, unable to get comfortable. He paced to the window and drew back the thick gold-and-ivory curtains to peer at the street below. The shop had been closed for over two hours, and the rush-hour traffic had slowed to a quiet flow of residents and the customers of nearby restaurants. No sign of Devin.

He let the curtains fall back, then leaned forward to check the old mantel clock once again. He'd never realized how much its constant ticking resembled the loud, thudding cadence of a military drum. *Tick. Tick. Tick.*

The surveillance monitors hissed.

Michael strode into the tiny kitchen and began to put away the dishes he'd washed after his supper. A plate on the shelf, some mismatched silverware in a drawer, his favorite coffee cup on a hook, and he was done. Maybe he'd make more coffee, he decided, yanking at the silverware drawer again. Wood groaned against wood, and the loose jumble of forks, spoons, and knives clattered, but somewhere beyond that rattle, Michael thought he heard a noise.

He raised his head to listen for someone coming up the stairs. Nothing.

He scooped the coffee into the machine, then turned on the tap to fill the pot.

There it was again. A noise. A clunking. Or was it a clanging? No, it was heavier than that. He turned off the water, but all he heard was the *tick, tick, tick* of the clock and the static hum of the monitors.

Perhaps Devin was having trouble getting the door that led to the apartment stairs open. He peeked out the kitchen window for any sign of the boy. No Devin.

"He probably just lost track of the time," Michael said aloud, hoping if he heard the words, he'd actually find them reassuring.

He filled the pot and poured the water into the machine, then leaned back against the kitchen counter to wait for the coffee to brew. "Yeah, he's probably hanging about, stalling."

What kid wouldn't choose hanging around with a friend over a tutoring session with a man he despised, anyway? He might even try, or at least consider trying, to hide out and then scoot home at the prescribed time, letting his mother believe he'd gone to the session as planned. Devin certainly had his reasons to avoid Michael.

But, being a good kid, he would eventually show up. Michael had no doubt about that. Unless there was something more serious than a case of hooky involved.

Michael glanced at the telephone. At what time should he be worried enough to contact Fiona? He, of all people, did not want to throw her into an unnecessary panic because Devin wasn't where he should be.

Guilt gripped him. His callousness of the past came back to haunt him in a wave of sickening regret. What a jerk he'd been. No matter how thorough his justifications—that he'd treated the boy well and had been acting, in the long run, in Devin's own interest by reclaiming his heritage—kidnapping the boy to get his hands on that gold was inexcusable.

That Fiona had forgiven him was a testimony to the depths of her Christian walk and the sincerity she invested in her friendships. That she cared for him as more than a friend was nothing short of a miracle, to Michael's way of thinking.

Thoughts of Fiona warmed his heart for a moment, pushing out the concern for Devin's whereabouts.

When he was young, he'd loved Fiona as a young man did, with energy and angst and longing and levity. He thought of the fun they had shared and of the pain in her eyes the day he chose the gold over her love.

He hung his head and raked both hands through his hair. Then he filled his coffee cup and moved out of the kitchen, back to the love seat. He set the cup aside, slumped down, and pushed out a cleansing sigh.

He and Fiona had been just kids then. What had they really known about love, anyway?

He'd asked that rhetorical question a thousand times over the years, and the answer came back the same each and every time: They must have known something because the love he'd felt for her then had not diminished with the passage of years.

He loved Fiona. He always had. And now, through the gift of time and the grace of God, she cared for him, too. He dared not hope she loved him, but he did hope that someday…

He shook off the mix of hope and nostalgia that threatened to overcome him. He had other things that demanded his immediate attention now. Such as where on earth was that Devin O'Dea?

His gaze moved to the clock again. He'd give that boy ten more minutes to show and then—

"Oh, no. Tell me it's not so." A movement on the right-hand

monitor caught his eye and chilled his senses. "Devin, don't tell me that that infernal gold has made a thief out of you, too."

"Don't ask questions, Fiona. I don't have the time or the frame of mind to answer them. Just get down to the shop and get down here fast." That was all Michael had said to her before hanging up.

Fiona's pulse raced as she imagined all the possibilities that frantic call could portend. Had her son been hurt? Had Devin and Michael quarreled so fiercely that Michael felt only she could mediate? Or was there a problem with the shop itself?

No. If Devin had been injured, Michael would not have kept it from her. If there were an emergency with the shop, he'd have called Gadberry. It had to be a problem between Devin and Michael.

Fiona curled her fingers around the steering wheel until her knuckles went white. Could her plan for throwing together the two people she loved most have backfired? Had she just set all of them up for a huge disappointment—or worse? And over what?

One lousy gold coin. A coin that, by her brother-in-law's account, held little significant economic value, and yet it had already cost her family so much. Had cost her so much.

Her gold ring dug into her finger as she turned the wheel to make a hard right. Lifting her chin, she pushed down the old fears and feelings that thoughts of the gold always produced. She'd done the right thing, she told herself as she drove through the quiet twilight, in keeping that coin from Michael.

Devin! She blinked, a flash of alarm speeding her heart rate over her slip-up. Keeping that coin from *Devin,* that's what she'd meant. She had done the right thing in keeping the coin from—

Michael. She relaxed her grip on the steering wheel, actually feeling relieved to finally admit the truth, if only to herself. When she had kept the coin from Devin, she had, for all intents and purposes, kept it from Michael.

That was how she had protected her heart. By controlling the last remaining coin, she had prevented Michael from getting the gold and ensured that he would never get the chance to choose it over her again.

Furthermore, she had allowed Devin to harbor great resentment toward Michael over the whole matter, hoping their bond would prove strong enough to overcome the difficulty. She'd gambled that the two of them could work things out because she trusted her son's relationship with Michael more than she did her own.

Fiona wasn't proud of her actions or emotions, but she still didn't know if she had the strength to change them.

She pulled her car into her usual space in the shop's back lot and cut the engine. Before she could gather her things, much less her thoughts, Michael was standing beside the car.

He pulled open the door. "Hurry."

"Hurry? Where? Why?" Her tennis shoes scraped over the gravel lot as he dragged her along faster than her stride could carry her.

"He got in through the back door—"

"He? Got in?" Rocks bit into the soles of her shoes, and she dragged her feet to slow down. Maybe this wasn't about the gold or about the strained situation with Devin. She took two steps to Michael's one, trying to catch up with him mentally as well as physically. "What are you saying, Michael? Was there someone in the shop? A break-in?"

He seemed to take her quickened pace as permission to move faster. "I caught him on the monitor just before I called you."

She stumbled. Jerking her arm free of his hold, she gave an aggravated huff and stopped. "Okay, let me see if I've got this so far. You observed a break-in on the security monitor and after that called me. Right?"

"Fiona, we're wasting time." He held out his hand, and when she didn't take it immediately, he stretched it farther to try to snag her forearm.

"Slow down, will you?" She maneuvered out of his reach. "First tell me, is anything missing?"

He moved close enough to place his hand on her back, applying pressure to propel her forward. "Not yet."

"Not yet?" Fiona resisted. "Michael, you don't mean he's still in there?"

"I wasn't about to let him go, especially not until you got here to deal with it."

"Me? What are you—" She blinked and shook her head. "Shouldn't the police be here? What about the alarm?"

"It didn't go off. My guess is he still had a key from when we cleaned out the storeroom a few weeks back."

"A key from…" Her cheeks burned and a sharp intake of breath stung her throat. "You mean Devin?"

"He's rummaging through the shop even as we speak, Fiona." He swept one hand back through his hair, leaving a disheveled mass of dark red waves in its wake. Fiona knew he did that when he worried, and from the tousled state of his hair right now, she guessed he'd fretted plenty about how best to handle the fiasco her son had just created.

"He hasn't taken or broken a thing as far as I can tell," Michael said. "He's just searching the store. I think I know what he's after, though I'm not completely certain."

She tipped her head back and put her hand upon his arm. "I know what he wants."

"It's the gold, then, isn't it?"

She nodded. "I told him about the last piece and that I'd locked it up here. He's probably looking for the combination to the safe."

"That's what I figured. I guess the only question now is what are you, as his mother, and me, as the shop's security guard, going to do about it?"

Looking into those eyes and seeing the genuine concern for her son, Fiona knew she'd been wrong not to trust him. He'd tried to teach Devin through the gift of the coin cross about a person's treasure. Now she understood that, just as Michael and Neal had made finding the coins their treasure and Cameron had made returning the coins his, she had made keeping the gold away hers.

"Michael, do you recall that day, fifteen years ago, when I told you I could never marry you?"

"You have a very diplomatic way of putting it, darlin' girl." He stepped close and stroked his thumb across her cheek. A sad smile tugged at his lips while his eyes glowed with a sweet, familiar warmth. "But the answer is, yes, I do recall it—and with a very heavy heart indeed."

She moved close enough for him to take her in his arms and bowed her head. "That day you told me that you could have everything you ever wanted on this earth if you could get your hands on one gold coin."

His hands were tentative on her shoulders. "Yes."

"I can't believe I'm saying this, but, Michael—" She pressed her palms to his chest and drew in a deep breath. "For the sake of my son and for the only hope that you and I can have a future together…I am going to give Devin his coin and allow him to do what he will with it."

Eleven

———

With one shoulder pressed to the shop's back door, Fiona placed her hand on Michael's chest.

His gaze dipped to where her hand rested, then he raised his face.

She felt his heart pounding beneath her palm, and the hard, steady beat made her own pulse pick up. Or was something else awakening the spark within her?

She lifted her chin.

His eyes flashed.

She wet her lips.

"Fiona?"

"Hmm?"

"If we expect to do this right, we'd better—"

"Yes?" She stretched up on her toes.

"Go inside and take care of Devin."

"Dev—?" She went as flat-footed as her spirits. "Oh, yes, that's right. Devin."

He placed his hand on the door and pushed it open without making a sound. "Are you ready then?"

She grabbed him by the arm. "Michael, wait."

He hesitated.

"Let me do this on my own," she whispered.

"Fiona, this shop is my responsibility."

"It's not as though you have to go in and play security guard." She nudged the door open just a crack to spy inside.

Her voice breathy and barely audible, she said, "It's only Devin, after all."

"You want me to stay outside because you don't want me anywhere near the gold until it's absolutely necessary, isn't that it?"

She froze, twisted her head to stare at him, and blinked. "No, Michael. That's not it at all. I only thought that alone I could sneak in easier and catch him off guard."

"Don't you think that'll scare the poor fellow?"

"Within an inch of his life, I'm hoping." She smiled.

Michael chuckled. "Are you sure you don't want my help?"

She liked that chuckle. She liked that Michael thought about how Devin would react. She liked having someone there to share this trying part of being a parent as well as the good times.

"Oh, all right, then," she said with a sigh. "Come on in with me."

He moved close behind her, one big shoe scuffing the gravel.

She frowned at the offending foot. "But for heaven's sake, be quiet!"

"As a church mouse," he promised.

"And stay close."

"Anything you say, darlin' girl. Anything you say."

He put his hand on her back, and together they crept inside the darkened storeroom.

Devin was muttering to himself as he rummaged through the drawers beneath the sales counter in the deserted shop. He was making just enough noise that he did not hear Fiona tiptoe in and manipulate the simple three-digit code on the small security safe in the back room.

Michael's eyes adjusted quickly to the dim light provided by the fading sunset. After Fiona found the coin, the two of them moved to the doorway.

Fiona stood there, with Michael so close behind that a wayward curl tossed back from her bright red hair clung to his T-shirt. He could hear her controlled breathing.

She lifted the single gold coin pinched between her thumb and forefinger and finally spoke up. "Is *this* what you're looking for?"

The boy whirled around. He gasped at the sight of his mother, then quickly focused on the gold piece.

"Is that what I think it is?" Hushed awe subdued his tone.

Michael felt the tension stiffening Fiona's spine.

"That's it? Just get straight to the gold, then?" She curled the gleaming coin into her fisted hand, which she kept raised. "Not even the pretense of remorse for breaking into a place of business?"

"I…I didn't break in. I had a key and—"

"You'll only make it worse if you try to justify it, son." Michael, avoiding eye contact with the boy, leaned over to flick on the front shop lights. "You know you weren't expected to be in here tonight and that you have no right to be going through things, key or no key."

The overhead light buzzed with the surge of electricity.

Devin thrust out his chin. "I have a right to get what's mine, don't I?"

An almost eerie fluorescent brightness blinked on, then off again from above them.

"Not at any cost, son." Michael met his gaze and spoke from the very core of his being. "Not if it hurts someone you love."

The light came fully on, humming with energy.

"I didn't mean to hurt anyone." Devin leaned back against the sales counter, his head down but his jaw still set in defiance. "I just came for—"

"This." Fiona held out the coin to him.

He did not lift his head to meet her gaze. "You mean you're…you're giving it to me?"

"If you want it badly enough to do this kind of thing, Devin, I don't think I have a choice. I won't live the next few years until you're an adult always mistrustful of what you might do to get your hands on this one worthless token."

His hand went out, palm up, open. But he hesitated. "It's not worthless."

"I guess that depends on how you define the term," she said, her words nearly void of emotion. "I'd say that something that weakens the bonds of trust between you and me is not something I'd value very much at all."

The boy's gaze darted away, but Fiona could still see the regret in his eyes. His chin trembled, then pushed up firm as his mouth set in a line. "I'm sorry about using the key to get in and look for the safe combination, Mom, but—"

"Sorry isn't enough in this case, young man." Fiona gestured with the coin in her hand. "You'll not get off scot-free for this little escapade tonight."

"Yes, ma'am." His hair fell forward over the bridge of his nose.

"You'll return the shop key, and as a punishment, you'll come here every day after class to do chores until it's time for your tutoring lessons or until the shop closes."

He frowned. "But Mom—"

"*Every day,* young man, until the summer-school session is over," she said. "Is that clear?"

His mouth twitched, and he bumped the heel of his tennis shoe against the counter. "Yes, ma'am."

"Beyond that, there are some things I want you to know before I give you this coin."

Michael watched the boy's expression move from humble

contrition to edgy anticipation.

"I don't do this lightly, you know, Devin." She rubbed her thumb along one notched edge of the coin in her hand. "And before I do, I want you to understand *why* I'm doing it."

"Okay." It took great effort for Devin to put on a sober mask, but Michael doubted if Fiona realized that.

Michael realized it because he knew exactly how the boy felt. Despite everything, he himself found it hard to appear indifferent with the gold so near. Yes, he'd had the two coins that he made into Devin's cross, but he'd known from the start that he would not use those particular coins to reclaim the family honor and fortune.

But with this coin, Fiona was placing in her son's hands the power to do what so many Shaughnessys and O'Deas had longed for, and he knew how the boy felt about the matter. That made all the difference.

Fiona braced her back against Michael's chest. "I'm giving you this and the responsibility that goes with it because you've forced my hand and because I've come to understand, with Michael's help, that I can't stop you from feeling as you do."

With Michael's help. He inhaled the scents of Fiona's hair and the musty shop. The feelings he had for her, his emotions about what was about to happen, and the advice he'd given her to let Devin confront his misplaced loyalties all clashed within him. Still, he placed his hand on her arm to lend whatever support he could.

"If I try to keep the gold from you and try to keep you from using it to discover the truth about your great-grandfather, it could take over my life. And only postpone the inevitable. All the stories and dreams and drive to avenge the old wrongs are too deep in you, Devin. It's something you're going to have to deal with. I can only hope that the faith and love I've shared

159

with you help you to make the right decisions." She held out the coin to him again.

Devin wiped his palm down his jeans, then stuck it out. He looked at Michael, who met his gaze with a profound sadness. The cold delight he saw in the boy's eyes had once been in his own. Once?

His stomach clenched. To be truthful, something of that delight remained in him even now. He didn't want to watch Devin take that coin because something in him shared the excitement of finally having the gold within his grasp.

Devin splayed his fingers.

Fiona moved away from Michael, sighing. She laid the coin in her son's outstretched hand.

A slow, satisfied smile worked over Devin's features.

Michael put his arm around Fiona's shoulders and gave a squeeze. "You're doing the right thing," he whispered. "Give him some time to think it over, and Devin will do the right thing, too."

"It's mine, then?" Devin touched one fingertip to the coin almost reverently. "It's truly mine?"

Fiona turned her cheek to Michael's chest. "Yes. It's yours."

"To do whatever I please?"

"Whatever you think is right," Michael admonished. "There's a difference."

"I know that, Uncle Mike."

Fiona gripped at the fabric of his T-shirt sleeve.

"And I intend to do what's right with this thing."

Michael pressed his lips together.

"What should have been done years ago," Devin went on.

Michael felt his head shake without having meant to make the gesture. He said nothing.

"Dad told me exactly what to do if the O'Deas found the gold." He looked at Michael, his expression grave.

Michael's own father had shared with him his role should the O'Deas produce a single coin from the stolen cache. He knew what he had promised to do then, what he had once wanted so badly he set aside all sense of right and wrong to have the chance to do. Now he only wanted to walk away, to tell Devin that what the boy felt was right was no longer something he could pursue.

"Uncle Mike?" Devin held the coin out to Michael.

Michael found Fiona's gaze.

She wet her lips.

"Is this what you want?" He had to ask it. He would not jeopardize their relationship over the gold ever again.

"No," she admitted in a hoarse but sincere whisper. "But it's what has to be, Michael."

He put one finger beneath her chin. "Not for my sake, it doesn't."

"Yes, for your sake and for mine, as well as for Devin's."

"I don't understand."

"Just as I can't go on wondering what Devin might do to get the gold, I can't move on with my life worrying about you."

"About…me?"

"Yes." Her green eyes misted over with unshed tears. "I lived too long with a man whose dissatisfaction crept into every aspect of our family life. I can't do that again."

"Fiona—"

"I'm not saying that's where this relationship is headed," she rushed to add, her cheeks stung by a pink glow. "But until this matter of old family wrongs and stolen gold is finished, we can't hope to move forward as individuals or as a couple."

The woman he'd wanted and loved for most of his life was telling him to seize the only thing he had sought harder and longer than he had her affection. Why wasn't he thrilled?

He ran his hand through his hair and then along his neck, where his fingers tripped over the chain that held his cross. *For where your treasure is, there your heart will be also.*

Michael drew in a breath. "Fiona, I'm not sure I want to do this."

Devin stepped closer. "If you're worried that I'll get all greedy and lose my faith over this, you're wrong. It's not about that for me, Uncle Mike. For me, it's about doing something...for my father."

"I understand that, son." Michael managed a weak smile. "Believe me, no one understands better than I how much a lad might hope to become a hero in his father's eyes."

"Then you'll help me?" He held the coin out.

"What if I'm not strong enough to keep my perspective?" he asked softly, not meaning to get an answer from anyone but himself.

"You are," Fiona assured him.

He looked into her eyes and saw such faith shining there that he almost believed she knew for certain. He drew a deep breath and shut his eyes, knowing his answer did not lie in a woman's trust or in his own will, but with God.

He opened his eyes. "I'll help you, son, but on one condition." Even with a stipulation, the thought of what he had agreed to do was overwhelming.

"What is it, Uncle Mike?"

"I promised my own father, as he did his before him, never to use the coin to reveal the truth unless every surviving male of the Shaughnessy and O'Dea families was present."

"What do you mean?" Fiona asked.

"I mean that I cannot proceed with any of this until we're all together. This whole business will have to wait until we can meet with Cameron."

That would give him time to pray and consider this matter, Michael thought. It would also provide Fiona and Devin with the support they would need if he proved too weak to walk away from the lure of the gold and the promise of being his own father's hero, just once.

Twelve

T hat ought to keep Devin busy for quite a while."
Fiona and Michael stood in front of the candle-making
booth, which Devin's youth group was manning for the
church's outdoor crafts fair.

"I have to admit," Fiona said, "I'm grateful for anything that
prevents him from asking me forty times a day when his Uncle
Cam is coming over."

"Are you beginning to regret telling him that Cameron
promised to spend time with him soon?"

She pushed back a strand of windblown hair and crinkled
her nose in the glare of the bright June sun. "No, I couldn't
very well keep it from him. He was just too excited about the
gold."

Michael nodded.

She wished she could read more into his quiet expression,
but she simply had no idea what went on in his mind these
days. It had been just over a week since she'd given Devin his
gold piece and, at Michael's request, had allowed the boy to
hang on to it. She didn't know if Michael secretly hoped the
boy would lose it or just lose some of his fascination with it by
seeing it daily. Devin had done neither.

She sighed and reached into her pocket to pull out a pair of
sunglasses. "Anyway, Cameron said he should have some free
time by the end of the week."

"I don't know if Devin can wait a week."

You don't know if Devin can wait—or if you can? The unasked question wedged in her mind and caused a dull ache in her chest. Michael had done nothing these last few days to make her think he'd lapsed back into his old ways. Yet she could not shake the memory of the look in his eyes when Devin held out that coin.

So much lay on the line now, as much or more than before, because not only was her precious child at stake, but so was her heart. She'd had it broken once by this man and these circumstances. Now, although she was older and her faith in God was stronger, her trust was weakened.

As much as she hated to admit it, the fact that she never seemed to get answers to her prayers, while Michael always seemed to get them, had colored her trust in God and in people. She felt new reluctance to turn her problems over to the Lord, and she worried that that might become a permanent way of thinking if she lost everything again.

Yet she had to risk it one more time. She swallowed hard. Was that really the right thing to do?

She studied the man standing next to her. The high noon sun created glinting highlights in Michael's deep auburn hair and accentuated the lines in his face. The open collar of his sports shirt made a V just low enough to reveal the top of the gold cross he wore.

Michael turned and smiled at her. He extended his hand. "What do you say you and I go browse through the craft booths?"

She looked down at her own hand. The gold ring on her finger winked in the sunlight. She continued to wear it heart pointed out to show that her heart had not yet been won. She blinked.

"Fiona?"

She inhaled. The air smelled of fresh grass, flowers, and all

166

kinds of food. Sounds of laughter and chatter and music surrounded them. She looked up into Michael's eyes.

"What do you say, Fiona?" He shifted his empty palm toward her. No guile, no secrets greeted her in his gaze. "The Lord has given us a lovely Saturday afternoon, and Mr. Gadberry's generous offer to tend the shop has given us the freedom to enjoy it."

The mention of Gadberry reminded her of Michael's refusal to take the promotion, despite Gadberry's insistence that he was the *man* for the job. Michael had been offered so much, but he'd turned it down because he put Fiona and her feelings ahead of personal gain. She lifted her shoulders to savor the sun's caress on her back. God had given them a glorious day and more hope and opportunity than she often appreciated, she realized.

A lightness filled her and burst through the surface of her uncertainty. She grinned broadly, her doubts evaporating. Trusting this man and God's goodness was the right thing to do.

She placed her right hand in Michael's and moved close to him. "I'd love to."

They strolled among the booths, sometimes stopping to admire a ceramic mug or a display of baskets. Once or twice Michael let go of Fiona to pick up a craft item or to greet a fellow church member. But he always found her hand again and fit it into his, as though that was where it had always belonged.

And each time Fiona eased out a sigh of contentment, Michael was filled with joy.

After all these years, Fiona was with him again and, God willing, they would now find the happily-forever-after they'd denied one another so long ago.

"Well now, isn't that a fine kettle of fish!"

Fiona's disgruntled tone startled Michael, and he looked up. "That's neither a kettle nor a sea catch," he teased. "It's just another craft booth."

He started to stroll away, suspecting where she intended to guide the conversation and knowing it was a place he did not want to go.

"Not just any craft, though, don't you see?" She stepped up to a booth with a royal blue-and-white striped awning flapping just above Michael's head and glanced over the inventory of rings and bracelets. "It's a jewelry designer. And look here; he seems to be doing quite well for himself in his trade."

"How nice for him," Michael muttered, purposely looking out at the shuffling crowd.

"Quite nice." She lifted up a simple silver bracelet and twisted the price tag around for Michael to inspect.

He caught the gesture from the corner of his eye but went on gazing at the hustle of the fair.

Fiona jabbed him in the ribs with her elbow, a gesture he could hardly ignore.

"Isn't this...exquisite?" She flashed the tag at him.

Michael took a reluctant peek, started, then squinted at it to make sure he hadn't imagined the number. He jerked his head up to smile at the craftsman behind the elevated glass display cases. "People actually pay these prices?"

The man chuckled good-naturedly at Michael's bluntness. "For unique, handcrafted jewelry, yes, they do."

Michael scanned the exhibit of the work with new interest as he rushed to assure the man. "It's beautiful work, truly beautiful."

"And he should know. He's a craftsman in the art himself." Fiona wrapped both hands around Michael's upper arm and gave it a squeeze.

"Ah." The man stroked his long, thinning beard. "Would I have seen you on the circuit?"

"Circuit?" Michael barely glanced up from his study of the rings, most of them silver, a few copper, and even some brass.

"The craft-show circuit," the man replied.

"Oh, no." Michael shook his head. "No, I don't sell my work. In fact, I haven't done much with it at all for many years now."

"Mmm." The fellow nodded as if to say, "Oh, a dabbler;" then he added a superior sounding sniff that all but said, "Probably isn't any good at it, either."

Or at least that was how Fiona must have taken it. She puffed up her chest and unwound her hand from Michael's arm. "Here's a sample of his work." She thrust her hand toward the man and wiggled her fingers. "Lovely, isn't it?"

The craftsman, who had been just about to turn away, stopped, cocked his head, then reached out to take Fiona's hand to bring the Claddagh up for a closer look.

"Nice." He leaned in even closer. "Very nice."

"'Twas done a very long time ago." Michael took Fiona's hand away. "I'm no longer doing that kind of thing."

"That's a shame, man, because you're very good."

"Good enough to make a decent living at it?" Fiona asked.

Michael gave her fingers a warning squeeze, but his look was playful.

"Decent? Yeah, I'd say that. If you could afford to work in gold and do pieces like that, you could skip the whole craft scene and sell through upscale stores." The man crossed his arms over his T-shirt. "If you're as good as that ring seems to indicate, you could do all right for yourself."

She gave a sidelong glance that held an "I told you so."

He answered with a hint of a sneer that said, "Don't start."

"I'm not doing this kind of thing anymore." He held up Fiona's hand locked in his. "But thank you for the compliment. I appreciate it coming from someone who does work of your caliber."

"You should see the cross he made for my son recently," Fiona continued. "He cut up these old gold coins and stuck them together to—"

"It's called metalsmithing, darlin' girl, not 'sticking them together.'" Michael took one half step away from the booth, tugging at Fiona. "And the man's not interested."

"Actually, I am."

"See?" She dug her heels in, which was an accomplishment considering she wore inexpensive canvas sneakers that squeaked and slipped on the freshly cut grass.

"I'd be very interested in seeing something like that, if you had it on you—"

"No, he doesn't," Fiona answered, her shoulders slumping.

Michael cleared his throat and scowled, as if it pained him to do so.

"You *do* have it on you?" She looked confused and glad at the same time. "That's great, but why?"

"I've made a practice of carrying it with me whenever I'm around Devin—you know, just in case."

A sweet softness came into her eyes that touched Michael's heart more than he would have expected. Clearly, his fondness for her son also deepened the sentiment Fiona felt for him.

"Would you—" She wet her lips, looking up at him from beneath her half-closed lashes. "Would you show it to the man, just to get an idea if it's the kind of thing that might sell? For me?"

Right then he'd have done almost anything she asked. Stifling a groan, he reached into his back pocket, pulled out his wallet, and flipped it open to retrieve the piece, which was wrapped in white paper.

"That's amazing," the man inside the booth whispered.

"It's actually very basic."

"But compelling." The man turned the piece over in his hand. "And very unique. Do you have anything else like it?"

"No." Michael held his hand out to take the piece back. "And it's unlikely I ever will."

"Why not?" The man's face hardened into a mask of pure concentration as he held on to the cross and continued to study it. "You said yourself that the style is basic. It can't be that difficult to recreate or to do something in the same vein."

"The style, yes, but the materials?" Michael's chest constricted. He straightened his spine and did not dare to glance at Fiona. "I no longer have access to the type of coins I originally used."

"That's a shame. They really make the piece—but maybe you could use something similar."

"You're that convinced it would sell, even if it were made of another type of material?"

"I'll show you how convinced I am." He bent down below the table of his booth and came back up with two business cards and an instant camera. He handed the cards to Michael and explained, "I carry this camera with me to shows to take pictures of really expensive pieces that people might want to think about before buying. I give them a picture to take with them and nine times out of ten they come back carrying that picture and want to make the purchase—or they call me at my studio to place an order."

Michael and Fiona exchanged glances.

"You keep one of those cards and write down your name and number on the other for me." He set Devin's cross down against the black velvet backdrop of his display cloth and put the camera to his eye. "I'll stick this picture in my case and see how much interest it draws, then contact you after the fair ends to let you know."

Michael glared at the card in his hand.

Fiona poked his upper arm with a pen.

He frowned but took it and scrawled his name and number across the beige paper.

The camera flashed.

Michael flinched.

The motor whirred, spitting out the black square of film. The man lifted the cross, removed the picture hanging from the end of his camera, then delivered the piece back into Michael's waiting palm.

"But you have to promise me this," the man said, waving the developing picture as he spoke. "If I should have some serious interest in this cross, you *will* consider doing some pieces on consignment with me."

The summer sun scored over the gold piece in Michael's hand.

Fiona edged near, her face filled with encouragement and anticipation of what Michael might say.

Slowly, like a man who has just taken a beating, he rewrapped the necklace, tucked the cross and the card into his wallet, and put the wallet into his pocket.

At his side, Fiona stood silently, obviously wanting to say something but holding back.

Years ago it had been her dream that he use his talent and give up his quest for family vengeance. He'd done half that and had been rewarded by her forgiveness; if he did the rest, could he hope to win her love? On that prospect alone, he smiled.

"All right, Mr.—" He flipped over the second card still in his hand and read, "R. J. Coleman. If you find there's enough inter-est in my work, give me a call, and we'll talk about what I can do to go into the jewelry-making business."

Michael handed him the card with his name and address written on it, and they closed the deal with a handshake. After they turned away, Michael asked with a genuine smile, "So, are you happy now?"

Happy? She rotated the ring on her finger to one side and smiled down upon the symbols of love, friendship, and fidelity.

Happy didn't begin to cover the range of emotions twining around one another inside her. Happy, scared, excited, elated, relieved, surprised—all of them and a few more she couldn't quite define vied for her attention. But she settled on one.

"I'd like to say I'm...optimistic."

"Is that better or worse than happy?" His brow creased.

She fiddled with her ring again, then met his gaze. "Better, I think."

"Well, then—optimistic it is." Michael dropped his arm to her waist and drew her near.

When they'd browsed among all the booths, Devin asked if he could stay a bit longer to help out, since their booth had proved far more successful than they'd expected. Fiona gave her permission gladly, pleased to see her son working so hard for a worthy cause—not to mention allowing herself more time with Michael. They found a shady, private spot under a big oak tree, where they sipped lemonade and listened to the leaves overhead rustle in the gentle breeze.

"I suppose you think I behaved rather badly today." She set her paper cup aside. "The way I forced you to talk to that man at the jewelry booth."

"Forced me?" He laughed and leaned back on one elbow, his long legs stretched out past the shade, toward the sunshine and the clutter of booths and people just beyond their quiet spot. "I'd hardly say you *forced* me."

Fiona pulled her legs up close to her body and looped her arms over her knees. "I did ask you to show him the cross you made for Devin."

"That you did."

She sank her teeth into her lip, wondering if she truly had the courage to guide the conversation as she wished it to go.

Michael glanced over at her, then reached out to brush a stray curl from her temple.

Her pulse leaped. She'd find the courage. "And I did show him my ring, which got it all started."

She extended her hand to draw his attention to the Claddagh ring.

Michael narrowed one eye at her. "Are you after something, darlin' girl?"

"After?"

He touched one finger to her nose. "I'm guessing you're angling to get a commission should I actually go back into the jewelry business."

"I...I..." She shook her head, her left hand pressed against her chest.

He gave her a sour expression.

"Oh, Michael, I wouldn't. I—"

Then he winked.

"Oh, you." She slapped his arm. "Just for that, I have half a mind not to tell you what I really was going to talk to you about."

"Tell," he coaxed, inching closer.

"I don't know...." She fingered her ring again.

"It's about the jewelry, isn't it?"

"It's about my ring."

"Your ring?"

"Yes." She heard her pulse building, and her hand trembled.

"What about it?" He took her fingers in his.

"I was thinking about its meaning."

"Its meaning?" He sat up, his curiosity obviously piqued. "Personal or traditional?"

She smiled down on the heart, its point still outward, the crown, and the two delicate hands on either side. Then she found his gaze. "Both."

His expression grew serious. "Fiona, are you thinking you should take off the ring? Is that it?"

She ducked her head. "Yes."

"I see."

He managed to fit a lot of disappointment into those two words, which only urged Fiona on.

"I think I should take it off." She lifted her head. "And then put it back on again."

"Do you mean…?"

She tugged at the circle, but before it budged, his fingers moved to help her.

"Here, let me." He slid the ring easily from her hand. He held it for a moment between his thumb and forefinger, then leaned in so close she could see the way his eyes dilated. "Fiona, I don't dare hope…but I have to ask."

Her gaze dipped to his mouth, then met his eyes again.

"Right hand or left?"

Instinctively, she put her right hand to her chest while the left went behind her back. "It's too soon. I'm sorry if—"

"It's quite all right." He reached out to take her right hand. "It's more than enough that you would wear my ring in a way that says your heart is taken. More than enough—for now."

He worked the ring back into place, this time with the heart turned inward. With her hand still in his, he leaned in closer and placed a kiss upon her lips.

Happy? Yes, she was that and so very much more. Fiona couldn't remember ever feeling so relaxed and able to abandon her life's worry, if just for a few hours. This day was a precious gift, and nothing, but *nothing*, was going to spoil it.

"Well then, what's this all about?"

Fiona nearly jumped from her skin at the sound of Cameron's voice. She turned to see him standing next to the tree. But he wasn't alone. Julia Reed, the homeless shelter director who'd been innocently tangled up in their family drama, stood next to him.

"Cameron, how did you find us here?" she asked as Michael got to his feet to extend his hand to his old friend.

"Don't ask him a question like that! He's liable to tell you it's some top-secret trick he learned in spy school." Julia laughed and gave Cameron a more-than-just-friends look.

Cameron gave her a wink and smoothed back his thick, golden hair.

Michael reached down to help Fiona up.

She slapped at her pants to dust herself off, then folded her arms and dipped her chin at Cameron. "Oh, I learned my lesson about dealing with this one years ago, Julia. I know perfectly well that he just let himself into my apartment with the spare key and saw the church flyer on the kitchen table."

Cameron leaned in toward Fiona to place a kiss on her cheek. "Have you ever thought about going to spy school yourself, lass? You'd make one fine detective."

"Says the man who needed me to read the road map to get us here," Julia said, offering her hand to Fiona after Cameron moved back.

Fiona clasped the strong hand in her small one and felt a

genuine warmth radiate between them. However, she noticed that Julia did not offer her hand to Michael. He did not press it, but to their credit, they gave one another nods of recognition and murmured greetings.

Fiona knew that Michael had, with Cameron acting as go-between, given Julia a heartfelt apology for all he had put her through when he whisked her away, planning to use her as a hostage to get past the authorities once he had the gold. He had not physically harmed her, but he'd felt great shame in his actions and had let her know how much he regretted what he'd done.

Julia, being a compassionate soul, forgave him almost before the words were out of his mouth and immediately asked what she could do to help him.

Fiona smiled. She liked Julia Reed. And she liked the fact that Cameron liked Julia.

She watched them, standing close but not quite touching, stealing coy glimpses as if they might at any moment casually slip their hands together and sigh in pure contentment. Michael put his hand on her shoulder, and Fiona smiled again. She knew just how they felt.

"The point is not *how* we found you," Cameron said, "but that we did, and that, since sweet Julia has cruelly refused the pleasure of my company on the first Saturday night I've had free in weeks—"

"I have three tickets to a banquet that my assistant and I must attend," Julia rushed to explain. "My assistant swears his girlfriend will kill him if she doesn't get to be with him tonight, and I simply cannot run the shelter without him." She shot a look at Cameron. "And no wisecracks from you, Mr. O'Dea, about my running everything."

Cameron held his hands up, his eyes wide, as if making

wisecracks had been the furthest thing from his mind. "The only thing I have to say is that Julia's plans leave me with a free evening."

Fiona's heart skipped as he turned to look at her and Michael.

Michael gave her shoulder a squeeze to lend his support.

Cameron clapped his hands together and announced, "So, I don't see why we can't put the time to use and resolve—oh, about a hundred years of mystery and misery for our two families."

T h i r t e e n

T his is it!" Devin rubbed his hands together, the picture of anticipation and glee.

"Not so fast, young man," Fiona warned.

"But we've got the coin, and all the surviving O'Deas and Shaughnessys are gathered," Devin said, as he bounced up and down on the edge of the bed in Cameron's motel room.

They'd chosen to meet in the room at the pleasant but not too fancy motel just off Interstate 275. Neutral turf, Michael had called it, meaning, she believed, to make light of the unspoken tensions they all felt.

Cameron had quickly agreed to the plan, saying he thought they'd all be more comfortable if none of them were *too* comfortable. That is, a room with no personal attachments would keep them from getting distracted and, if they had problems, make it harder to say, "It's late; let's leave this here until tomorrow."

Fiona understood that this was only a slight psychological edge and that in reality, anything might happen tonight. Still, she was glad that whatever did take place, it would not happen in her home. If it went badly, she did not need that memory haunting her each time she settled into her living room. And if it went well...

Fiona's stomach knotted. She had no idea how it could go well. If this did, indeed, prove .hat the Shaughnessys and O'Deas had some claim on the money, it could throw her life into turmoil. It would mean that she and Michael would have to make choices she had believed were well behind them now. Making those choices could change the whole nature of their relationship—as it had once before.

And then there were her responsibilities to her son. How would she handle those if it turned out that the gold was really his family legacy?

Devin's gaze ping-ponged from one adult to the next. "Well, what are we waiting for?"

"It's not so much a matter of waiting, son, as it is a matter of everything in good time," Michael said. His long fingers drummed against the cardboard box under his arm.

"This is a hundred-year-old puzzle, my boy." Cameron settled into one of the two burnt-orange chairs in front of the closed drapes. "You don't expect us to be bringing the riddle to an end bing-bang-boom, do you now?"

Devin gulped in a breath, obviously preparing to launch a protest, but Cameron cut him off with a teasing glance at Fiona.

"Appears my nephew has lived in America too long," Cameron said. "He's forgotten the Irish way of doing things."

"What's the Irish way of doing things?" Devin asked, twisting his head to glance back at his mother, who was seated with her back against the headboard of the bed.

"Slow," she told him, trying to look stern.

"And lyrical," Michael added. He seated himself in the chair opposite Cameron, then slid the cardboard box onto the small round table in front of him.

Fiona noted that he kept his arm slung over the box. The gesture appeared casual, but she suspected it was anything but.

"We don't rush through business as important as this, son." Michael wagged one finger at the boy.

"Not when there are stories to be told," Cameron said.

"Stories?" Devin rubbed the heel of his hand against his temple as if to show that this postponement was giving him a headache. "What stories?"

"Family stories, lad." Cameron glanced at Michael and then at Fiona. "You cannot hope to understand the importance of what we are about to do without first understanding what led us to this point."

"My dad told me all about——"

"No," Cameron said sharply. "My brother and my father, they only knew a part of the story. No one O'Dea or Shaughnessy has ever known the whole of it."

"Why not?" Devin looked from Fiona to Cameron, and then to Michael.

Michael leaned forward, his eyes aglow with excitement and a hint of the old Irish mischief as he grinned at the boy and whispered, "Listen, son—and learn."

They all inhaled at the same time and, it seemed, held that breath. Michael and Cameron exchanged glances. Then Michael gave a short nod and cleared his throat.

"Since it began with a Shaughnessy, I'll start off the tale," Michael said. "The year was nineteen hundred, and my great-grandfather Kerwin Shaughnessy——"

"*Your* great-grandfather?" Devin perked up, already intrigued. "I thought this all started with my father's grandfather, *my* great-grandfather."

Michael smiled. "Ah, that's one of those things that you must understand before you agree to take on this family responsibility, son. You've heard us speak of the 'century-old crime,' haven't you?"

The boy nodded.

"Didn't it ever strike you as strange that if a man believed he

181

had a legitimate claim to the gold, he would refer to the taking of it back as a 'crime'?"

"I never thought of that," Fiona murmured. Suddenly she realized that for all the veiled allusions she'd heard to the local legend, of all the bold yarns and fanciful fabrications from childhood on, she really knew little of the true story.

"You see, son," Michael went on, "when we speak of the 'crime,' it's of an injustice done to young Kerwin long before any Shaughnessy befriended any O'Dea."

"What was it?" The boy scooted to the edge of the bed.

Fiona found herself drawn forward as well.

Michael spread his hands open as if he could tamp down the prickle of tension in the room. "Understand, son, that I can only tell as was told to me."

Cameron folded his hands together and kicked his boot up to rest on his knee. "'Tis an old story passed from father to son for four generations, Devin, colored by time and emotions—to what extent, we'll probably never completely understand."

"I see." Devin's expression grew serious.

"Now, it all began with my great-grandfather Kerwin Shaughnessy," Michael began again. "He was never a poor man, not in comparison to many of his area. He had a trade. As far back as that, the Shaughnessys were practicing the craft of metal-smithing. 'Tis said we have a gift for it."

Fiona bowed her head and wriggled her ring finger.

"Take note of that, Devin," Cameron said. "The skill of the Shaughnessys at their craft was celebrated throughout the area and would be still if—"

"If it were the kind of thing a man might make a living at," Michael interjected.

Cameron conceded the point with a tilt of his head but made no further comment.

Michael continued. "Now Kerwin, finding few opportunities to better himself in Ireland, had a dream of a place where he could rise above the poverty that surrounded him and use his hands to build a good life for himself and the family he would one day have."

Devin cocked his head, concentration lining his face.

"Kerwin spoke of this often. Of how he would someday leave his home and find this place, this dreamland that was one step away from paradise."

"America," Devin murmured.

Michael smiled. "Yes."

"It's how my father often spoke of it," the boy said softly.

"And mine," Michael said.

"Mine, as well," Cameron added.

"The seed was planted long ago," Fiona explained, touching her son's ankle lightly.

"So it was that Kerwin had his heart set on two things: the first, coming to America; and the second, a beautiful young woman."

"Oh?" Fiona had never heard this piece of the tattered old narrative. "There's a love story in this?"

"Something of one, yes." Michael's smile was only for her, fleeting but very tender. "Her name was Rose. Rose O'Mallory. And she was my great-grandmother."

He paused to let that sink in, then continued. "She was a beautiful lass with a fair face and a strong spirit, well loved by all who knew her and cherished like Solomon's own treasure by her wealthy, manipulative father."

"It already sounds like trouble," Fiona whispered to her son. She turned to Michael, a bit more caught up in the yarn than she'd intended to find herself. "What happened? Did her father forbid the match?"

Michael grinned. "Headstrong as he was, Rose's father had his weak spot—and that spot was squarely occupied by his sweet daughter. So when young Rose determined it was Kerwin she would marry and no other, her father agreed. But, as you can imagine, he despised the idea that Kerwin would someday take his lovely Rose away from him to the faraway shores of America."

Devin groaned and tossed his head back in a display of teenage melodrama. "I thought we were going to hear the story of the stolen gold, not all this mushy stuff."

"This *is* the story of the gold," Cameron said, laughing at the boy's antics. "At least the Shaughnessy version of it."

Michael resumed the tale. "Now, in those days no woman of any station would ever be given in marriage without a dowry. And Kerwin asked that Rose's be given in gold coins. He was very specific about that. It had to be gold, and it had to be coins. Gold because, as it was a part of his trade and talent, he understood its value and he knew how to tell if it was a fake. You see, he suspected Rose's father might try to trick him in some way. He also knew that gold was a currency that would take him to America and support him there while he established himself."

"Wait a minute!" Devin held up his hand. "I thought this whole thing started over a piece of land."

"Rose o' Mornin'," Michael said in near reverence.

"What?" Devin scrunched up his nose.

"Kerwin asked for gold because he knew he had to, but there was another way in which Rose's father got to keep both his daughter and his coins." Michael paused and looked into the distance.

Fiona sank her teeth into her lower lip. She couldn't help but wonder if Michael was thinking about how he, too, could keep the gold and the girl. She wanted to tell him not even to imagine it. She would not share her heart with that vile treasure ever again. Of course, she dared not speak at all. She merely waited until Michael blinked, shook his head, and returned to the story.

"The gold was Rose's dowry, but her father also gave a special wedding gift—the land. While Kerwin's wariness caused him to take precautions over the dowry, for all the good it eventually did him, he made no such provision for the land. He never saw nor signed a deed to the wee scrap of land that came complete with a fine white cottage, a barn, some hens, and one plow horse."

"Was *that* the crime?"

Michael nodded. "Rose's father let them believe they owned their own little bit of heaven on earth, the only thing that could, in Kerwin's mind, compete with the lure of America."

"So they never left Ireland," Fiona concluded.

Michael shook his head. "They called it Rose o' Mornin' after Rose herself and stayed there to make a home and have their children."

"What happened to the gold?" Devin scratched his head, leaving a bright red ruffle of hair in his wake.

"Always the thoughtful one, Rose's father took the gold coins back shortly after the wedding. Promising to keep them just as he'd presented them for her dowry, he placed them in a safe in his home." Michael glanced at the cardboard box on the table. "At least he thought he took back all the coins."

"You mean he didn't?"

Michael cocked an eyebrow. "Kerwin was a man of simple needs, son, not stupid. He kept one coin back so he could later match it up should any of the coins suddenly begin to circulate."

185

Fiona gasped. Just as she had never heard of Rose and Kerwin, she'd never known that there was one coin held out. Suddenly she understood Michael's claims that having a coin could prove his family's side of things. What had once been conjecture and fairy tale might soon turn to reality.

"And these are the same coins Uncle Cam and I dug up under the billboard?" Devin asked.

Michael and Cameron exchanged glances, then Cameron, his jaw tight, said, "That's one of the things we're going to find out tonight."

"But Michael," Fiona asked, "even if the coins match, will it be enough to get the gold back? Legally?"

He shrugged. "That remains to be seen."

The response only edged up her anxiety.

Michael laid his hand on the table next to the box. "Years passed, and Rose and Kerwin's family grew. Rose o' Mornin' became a fine home, but they never gave up the dream of America. They often spoke of that dream with their son, Brennan.

"Kerwin and Rose built up in Brennan a fierce desire to see this America. And then they gave him the means to do so by telling him that he could have the gold his grandfather held in trust when he became a man fully grown."

"Your grandfather?" Devin asked.

"Yes. That gold was now his birthright and his means of grasping his dreams."

"But he never got it," Devin said.

"He was never *given* it," Michael corrected.

"And that's where the O'Deas come into the story, lad." Cameron stood and stretched.

"What happened?"

Fiona opened her mouth to give what little information she

knew, but Cameron spoke up.

"I'll tell it," he said. "But first, do you suppose we could get some sodas in here? I hate to tell a story on a parched throat."

"No, you can't stop now," Devin protested.

"There's the American coming out in him again." Michael chuckled. "He wants everything all at once, no time to sit and mull it over. Just more, more, more."

"I wish this was a movie on videotape so I could fast-forward to the good stuff." Devin plunked his chin in his hand.

Cameron laughed, reaching into his pocket to pull out his wallet. "There's a soda machine just down the hallway, Michael, my friend. Care to stretch your legs a bit and walk with me?"

Fiona didn't know whether she or Michael was more surprised by the easy camaraderie Cameron showed toward the man who had gone from near brother to fierce adversary.

Michael raised his hand, she thought, to snatch up the cardboard box between them.

She wadded a bit of the quilted bedcover in her hand, wondering how Cameron would react to having his overture greeted with distrust. She wondered, her heart thudding, if having proof of the gold's ownership—if, in fact, it could be proven—had affected Michael already.

"Here, then, help me out of this chair." Michael stretched his hand past the box. "I don't recover quite so quickly as I used to from sitting about spinning tales."

Cameron's hand clasped Michael's.

Though only a simple gesture, it warmed Fiona's heart and gave her hope that all would right itself.

The two men stood, and as Cameron pulled open the motel-room door, Devin leaped up as well.

"Aw, c'mon, guys, you can't leave me hanging like this," he whined.

His uncle gave a salute and a parting wink. "Just think of it as a pause for station identification."

"Huh?"

"Actually, Cameron, they don't say that anymore," Fiona said.

"They don't?"

"Here, let me try." Michael leaned against the open door. When he spoke, his voice was low. "We'll be right back after these brief messages."

"Very funny." Devin crossed his arms over his chest and pouted. "I'm never going to find out what happened with the gold, am I?"

"Oh, you'll find out soon enough, son." Michael stepped into the hallway.

"Before the night is over—we all will."

Cameron's chilling prediction rang in Fiona's mind after the two men had sauntered down the hall. She had hated what Michael did to Cameron, how he used Devin to try to get to the gold that she now knew had been Rose O'Mallory's dowry. But she had forgiven Michael through time and a purposeful rebuilding of trust. Now that she saw him and Cameron together, the remnants of her family, laughing and helping one another, she knew that the two men could repair their friendship as well.

Or at least they could at this moment. Her gaze fell on the ominous box. Who knew what would happen after Cameron told the rest of the story of theft and greed that eventually led some to prison, some to drink, and in the end, brought them all here together tonight.

Fourteen

Coins clinked through the slot and rattled inside the soda machine. "Nervous?"

Michael studied Cameron as Cameron studied the soft-drink selection. "I won't lie to you. I am a wee bit nervous, at that. And you?"

"I didn't think I would be. After all this time, after all I've put myself through—after what we've put one another through—I thought I had it all figured out. Under control."

Michael nodded. "At least now, whatever we discover, we'll be done with it."

Cameron turned his head to put his face in three-quarter profile, not meeting Michael's gaze directly but not avoiding it either. "Even if 'tis proven those coins I just returned are the real and rightful property of the Shaughnessy family?"

Michael could not answer. A year ago, even a few months ago, he would have known exactly what course to pursue should he finally uncover any hard evidence to his family's claims. Today...

Today he had Fiona to consider. She despised that gold, what it had come to stand for in her life, what it had cost her. If winning the gold meant losing her, he did not want it anymore. He understood that now, understood what he often wished he'd understood so many years ago when she first asked him to choose. He loved her, and that was more important than any of this gold nonsense could ever be.

"It'll probably surprise you to hear this, old friend—"

Michael broke off. "If I can still call you my friend, Cameron?"

"You can. You know that."

"Yes, I knew it even when I was half crazed over that blasted treasure. When I acted like such a…" He clenched his fist at his side, then relaxed it. "I want to thank you for how you handled that, Cameron. And what you did to make sure I didn't rot in jail."

"What *I* did? Devin's the one who weakened the case against you."

"You could have made a case, I'm thinking, if you had wanted to. But you didn't, and you didn't encourage your lady friend, Miss Reed, to, either."

At the mention of the lady's name, Cameron smiled.

There was a story there, Michael supposed, but one better left to another time. He sighed and reached into his pocket to pull free some change. "The point is, I want to thank you for all you did."

"And I want to make it clear that I didn't pull any strings, if that's what you mean."

"No, I meant the things you said to me. Your insistence even after all I'd done that I could find my way back to the truth. That the Lord was the way, not the gold." He ran the tip of his index finger along the chain around his neck. "I thought about that a lot while I was in jail. It reminded me of so many things I'd once known and cared about but then just let slip away."

"Are we talking about your faith or Fiona?" Cameron grinned.

"My faith." He tried not to give away his feelings for Cameron's sister-in-law. "My entire values system—that's what I had lost. But I've gotten it back."

"And Fiona, too?" Cameron raised one eyebrow, still grinning. Then, with only a quick glance in that direction, he punched one of the big, glowing buttons before fixing his unflinching gaze on Michael again. The vending machine thumped a couple of times, then sent a can rolling down. Cameron reached down to pick it up, still waiting for Michael's answer. "Well?"

"Yes, all right, and Fiona, too," Michael finally admitted. "I've renewed my faith in God and my interest in Fiona as well."

"And she shares this interest?"

Michael thought of their kisses and of the way she'd turned her ring to say that she accepted his affection. "Yes, she seems quite…interested."

"I thought something more was going on when I found you two at the craft fair. I just couldn't decide what it meant."

"Well, now you know." He shouldered Cameron aside to take his turn with the machine. "Are you happy?"

"Much more than I thought I would be," Cameron confessed, slapping his friend on the back.

When they returned to the motel room, they found Devin sprawled on his belly across the width of the bed, obviously prepared for a lengthy tale. Fiona, Michael noted, still sat at the head of the bed, her back just as stiff, her legs straight out in front of her, crossed at the ankles.

He'd dragged out his part of the story long enough, he decided, seeing her discomfort. Postponing the inevitable only grated on the already raw emotions running in the room. For Fiona's sake, Michael decided, he must get this done, neat and clean. Then they could deal with the consequences.

"All right, then." He handed a cold soda to Fiona and plunked his own next to the box on the little round table. "Let's see if we can't pick up the pace a little."

"Sure, when it's *my* turn to have the spotlight, you want to hurry things along," Cameron said, pretending to sulk.

Devin laughed.

Even Fiona smiled a bit.

Michael perched on the edge of his seat, holding the stinging cold can by the rim. "I'll hurry along my part of the tale, then hand it over to you. Mind you, though, we won't stand for any great theatrics. No weeping or wailing. No pounding of your chest or any of that type of folderol."

"'Folderol' indeed." Cameron snorted. "'Mr. Rose o' Mornin'—a 'wee bit of heaven on earth.'" He lifted his face and pretended to wipe a tear from the corner of his eye.

Devin laughed again.

Michael joined him.

"You just be brief with what you have to say." Cameron sat back and rolled his eyes. "And never you mind about my part in the matter."

"Fine." Michael stole a peek at Fiona, glad to see that the good humor seemed to have some effect on her. She wasn't smiling exactly, but she didn't look quite so much like a deer caught in the headlights of an oncoming car, either. "Now, where was I?"

"Brennan hoped to use the gold to come to America," Devin rushed in to remind him.

"Ah, that's right." Michael tapped the top of his soda can. "Now, you'll recall that Rose's father dealt with business matters in something of a…creative way."

"He was a crook," Cameron muttered.

"Are you telling this or am I?"

"*You're* the one who said he wanted to hurry this thing along."

Michael harrumphed at his friend, then turned back to Devin. "He was a crook."

A sharp pop and fizz as Cameron opened his drink underscored the sentiment.

"A crook," Michael went on, "who eventually got caught owing a great deal of money to the government. The details about all this are very sketchy since this downfall took place many decades ago."

"When was it?" Devin asked.

"In the 1920s—Brennan was around sixteen, I believe. Rose's father lost almost everything, including Rose o' Mornin'."

"Is that when Rose and Kerwin found out they didn't own the land?" Fiona asked.

"Indeed. They lost their home, their livestock, everything, because it had never truly belonged to them. But they did not lose hope."

"Sure they didn't," Devin muttered. "They had a bunch of gold."

"Or so they thought. But when they went to retrieve their gold from Rose's father, it had vanished. And not a soul heard or saw another thing about it for the next twenty-five years." Michael pulled back the tab on his can, and the soda hissed and popped.

"That's when the O'Deas entered the picture."

Devin sat up at Cameron's remark. "Finally."

Cameron laughed. "It was now about 1950, and my grandfather, Owen O'Dea, had taken a day's labor on the farmland once known as Rose o' Mornin'."

"Where were Kerwin and Rose?" Fiona asked.

Michael smiled at her, glad to see that romance still had a place in her heart despite the apprehension in the air. "You needn't worry, Fiona. Kerwin and Rose found a new home, began again, and lived happily until their deaths in the late 1940s."

"Oh, good." She blew a tiny breath between her lips, her response making Michael long to reach over and steal a small kiss.

He resisted.

"Now, Owen was…" Cameron wrung his hands together, his gaze focused upward as if the right term might suddenly fall from the ceiling. "Well, let's just call him a dreamer."

"Couldn't hold a job," Michael translated.

"That too." Cameron took a long sip of his soft drink, then set the can down. "'Tis true that Owen did not hold steady work, but he did take the odd job now and again to tide his family over. Now on this particular day, for some reason I've never heard tell, the job he'd found himself doing was digging."

"He didn't!" Devin grabbed his sides and rolled onto his back, groaning. "He dug up the gold!"

"You've got it, son," Michael said, smiling at the boy's antics.

"Go, Owen." Devin sat back up, targeted Cameron with a stare, and asked, "Then what?"

"What do you think? The town ne'er-do-well hauls up what seems a fortune in gold coins? The town still talks about the stir it created."

"Was it totally wild?" Devin turned around to look at Fiona.

She frowned. "How would I know? I wasn't even born in 1950."

"You weren't?" Devin's tone was one of disbelief.

"Just how old do you think I am, young man?" Fiona paused for a heartbeat before saying, "Cancel that question. I don't want to know."

Cameron and Michael struggled to conceal their amusement, but neither succeeded. She glared at them.

"Of course, as soon as Brennan heard of it, he knew it was Rose's dowry," Michael said.

"As you might imagine," Cameron continued, "Owen immediately disputed Brennan's claim to the money—possession being nine-tenths of the law and all."

"Wait," Devin said. "I thought they were partners."

"What happened next made them partners," Cameron said.

"What happened?" Devin scooted close.

"Now, I'm not sure of the man's position—I've heard he served on the county council, and I've heard otherwise as well," Cameron continued. "But a man of some prominence—"

"Tom Finney." Michael did not realize until after the name had left his mouth how harsh his tone was.

"Tom Finney," Cameron echoed quietly. "Finney interceded in the situation between Brennan and Owen. When Brennan swore he had a way to identify the coins as his mother's dowry, Finney deemed that someone, some impartial party, should hold the coins until Brennan could collect his proof and the dispute could be rightly settled."

"Finney volunteered," Devin guessed.

"He volunteered all right, but when they returned, Finney claimed he had turned the gold over to the proper authorities and they'd have to take it up with them. It all might have been over then and there as far as the O'Dea family was concerned if Finney hadn't already been in trouble."

"He was not a well-liked man." Michael kept his tone even this time. "And he'd done others wrong besides my grandfather. This incident only helped to fuel local anger toward him."

"As the American expression goes, the heat was on ol' Finney." Cameron clucked his tongue. "Not that this justified Shaughnessy and O'Dea's decision, but it wasn't too long before another scandal came knocking at Finney's door. Now, I don't know what that was, but word got 'round of how he intended to handle it—with a payoff."

"In gold?" Devin nodded as though he'd been onto the scheme from the very start.

"Untraceable gold, at that," Fiona whispered.

"Or so he believed," Michael corrected.

"'Twas then that Shaughnessy and O'Dea forged their bond—and hatched the plan we've each of us learned in turn at our fathers' knees," Cameron said.

"That's when they decided to steal the gold back," Devin said.

"Only they did not think of it as stealing," Michael said. "Because Brennan knew he had something that could completely vindicate their actions."

Michael set his drink aside, stood, and rubbed the dampness from his hands.

He felt everyone's eyes follow him. A low, growling rip shook the silence as he tore away the packing tape on the cardboard box he'd kept charge over since coming to America years ago.

He flipped back the top of the box, swallowed hard, and peered inside. It was filled with shredded paper. He closed his eyes for a moment and prayed a fleeting prayer that he would handle this well and with a true Christian perspective. Then, with his heart thumping like hoofbeats in his ears, he thrust his hands into the box.

His fingers brushed something hard and cold. He heard someone murmur something behind his back, but he could not make it out. He gritted his teeth, fit his fingers to the object, then tugged it free.

He held the small, battered silver box in both hands for everyone to see. "Brennan Shaughnessy convinced Owen O'Dea to take back the gold because he had this."

Fifteen

Cameron fell back in his chair and began to laugh.

Fiona gaped at his behavior. This was an emotionally packed moment. The sight of the box had caused a flutter in her stomach and a heaviness in her chest. Years of bitterness and disappointment were about to come to a head because of the evidence resting in that tarnished silver container. And all Cameron O'Dea could do was laugh?

"What's wrong with you?" Michael asked, his face set in a scowl.

"Nothing." Cameron sat up and sniffed. "I was just thinking how much your little theatrics there put me in mind of a sandwich."

"A sandwich?" Michael blinked at his friend.

Fiona blinked too.

"Yeah—blarney and ham!" Cameron slapped his knee and laughed again.

Michael winced.

Blarney and ham. Fiona tried not to smile too broadly at the comparison.

"Very funny." Michael's jaw tightened. "I guess I'm lucky you didn't call it 'cheesy,' too."

"Only 'cause I didn't think of it," Cameron shot back.

Fiona clamped her hand over her mouth but could not contain her sputtering giggle. "Actually, I thought the whole act was rather 'rye.' You know…wry?"

Devin looked at them all as if they'd lost their minds and

shook his head at Michael as though to say in his American way, "They are so uncool."

That must have done it for Michael, for at that moment his grim mask broke, and he joined in the tension-relieving laughter.

"Okay, so I indulged in some amateur showmanship," he admitted. "It's just that we've all waited so long for this moment, I felt I needed to make it something we could—"

"Relish?" Cameron said.

"Enough with the food jokes, already." Michael batted off the last pun with a wave of his hand. "Can we just get to this and get it done?"

Fiona sobered instantly. For the second time tonight, Michael had encouraged them to hurry. Was he that anxious to get his hands on the proof? If so, why? Because he truly wanted to put an end to this, or because his old greed had come back?

"All right, then." Cameron straightened in his chair. "Where were we?"

"Brennan Shaughnessy and Owen O'Dea hatched a plan to get back their gold," Devin said, his interest renewed.

"Years earlier Kerwin had fashioned this box to hold his important papers and what-have-you, including the gold coin he'd kept," Michael said, gesturing toward the silver box he set on the table. "Knowing he had his evidence, Brennan then forged a bargain with Owen that they would follow Finney, and when he made the payoff, they would show themselves and reclaim the gold."

"In other words, they decided to ambush Finney and *steal* the gold," Cameron said. "Which they did. But in order to keep from getting caught, they had to split up. Brennan took the evidence and Owen the gold, both realizing that one was no good without the other."

"Why?" Devin looked to his mother.

"I suppose because unless they could prove the gold was theirs, they couldn't ever spend it," Fiona said. "Which is why, I'm guessing, that even though the O'Dea family has known the whereabouts of the gold for some time, they couldn't do anything about it."

"That and the fact that they lived an entire ocean away from the gold." Cameron's lip curled, obviously none too proud of his family's role.

"I don't understand," Fiona said.

"'Twas that gold that brought you to America, Fiona, not dreams." Cameron clasped his hands in front of him, then released them. "Owen took the gold and ran with it, coming to America. When Brennan realized he'd been duped, he began to talk about what they had done, how he had been wronged. It didn't take long for Finney and his contacts to have Brennan arrested and Owen deported from America."

"They never got the gold back, and Brennan and Owen died in prison," Michael said.

"My father, with Neal's help, brought you and Devin here so they could search for the hidden gold." Cameron kept his head bowed as he spoke.

Fiona knew her father-in-law had felt this way, but she'd made herself believe that Neal would not have uprooted his family just for a chance at stolen treasure. Not that she wasn't happy with the move, but knowing that Neal's deepest motivation was the gold, not his family's welfare, made Fiona heartsick. Now more than ever, she wished she could excuse herself from this whole affair and forget the horrible treasure ever existed.

"Do you mean they just happened to build a lottery billboard with a rainbow on it over the spot where Owen had buried the gold?" Devin asked. "Cool!"

Her son's enthusiasm rattled Fiona's nerves.

"That's not how it happened, lad." Cameron managed a smile for his nephew. "My father and yours found the gold and moved it there, to keep it safe."

"Why didn't they just cash it in?" Devin asked. "There are lots of places you can get money for gold coins. I've seen 'em advertised on TV."

"Devin!" Fiona put a hand to her throat, feeling it closing as she listened to her son's reasoning. "Do you really think so little of your father and grandfather that you'd expect them to sell off something that did not belong to them?"

"No, son, all they wanted was what they considered the O'Dea share of the legitimate Shaughnessy money," Michael said.

"Then why didn't you just show them what was in that box and be done with it, Uncle Mike?"

"Because I couldn't open it." Michael picked up the box. "You see, while still in the planning stage, Brennan feared that Owen might just keep the money, and Owen feared that Brennan could show his evidence to the authorities and call Owen a thief. So they made this arrangement."

He tipped the box so they could see the small slot in the top of it. "Brennan, being gifted in metalsmithing, made a lock with the coin he had so that the box could only be opened with one of the original coins as a key."

"Since Owen had taken the gold, only Owen could supply the means to retrieve Brennan's proof," Cameron added.

"And so the Shaughnessys and O'Deas became entwined, which was why Cameron's father felt compelled to take me in during the times my own father could not care for me," Michael said softly. "And perhaps why Neal insisted a Shaughnessy become Devin's godfather, even knowing it made

Fiona uncomfortable, given our personal history."

"Neal cared for you like a brother, Michael." Cameron's eyes were somber.

"He did indeed." Fiona swung her legs over the edge of the bed but didn't stand. She doubted her legs would hold her at the moment. "I worried over the choice at first, but now..."

She did not finish. A wary silence hung over the room.

Finally, Devin wiggled impatiently on the bed, folded his arms, and asked, "If they had the box and the coins, why didn't Dad, Grandpa, and Uncle Mike just do what we're doing tonight?"

Fiona angled her chin up. "They were going to, weren't they?"

Michael's face went pale. "The night of the car accident, Neal and his father were coming to strike a bargain with me about sharing the gold. When I heard about the wreck, I was near crazy with regret for having even suggested the meeting, Fiona."

She had always suspected that the coins were in some way connected to her husband's death. They had been related to so much of the misfortune and tragedy that she had known throughout her life. She knew they held no special power, that they were only earthly things, but when men instilled in them such importance, then nothing good could come of it. Her gaze found Michael's.

His expression darkened with remorse. "I knew then I'd do whatever it took to make up for it, to help you and Devin in any way within my means."

Hot tears sprang to Fiona's eyes, but she lifted her chin to keep them from falling. "That's why you stepped in to take care of us after Neal died? Why you became like a father to Devin— out of guilt?"

"No, Fiona." He stood, pushing the box aside. "I came back into your lives because that's where I belonged. I had pledged long ago to care for Devin when he became my godson. I stepped in to fulfill my responsibility and then learned that I truly did love him like my own child."

"Your own child?" Fiona rose from the bed, her voice strained. "Is that why you kidnapped him?"

"I kidnapped him to get the gold, Fiona, but you have to understand?…" He reached out to brush his fingers over her arm. "If guilt drove me to anything, it was to get the gold. I thought I was doing it for Devin's sake—that I owed it to Neal to see that his son received his heritage."

"'Tis true, Fiona," Cameron said. "Whenever I spoke to Michael during that time, he always reminded me that he wanted the gold for Devin."

"*I* didn't want it for his future." She moved her arm from Michael's hand. "Why didn't you stop to think about that?" She blinked, and dampness bathed her cheeks. "In fact, I still don't want any part of this. Not for me or for my son."

"But, Mom, we're so close to finding out—" Devin's voice cracked.

"What? That this is some long-dead woman's dowry? And what if it is? It's the Shaughnessys' money and has nothing to do with us."

"It's due our family, too, Mom. Dad always said so. We earned our stake in it."

"How? By extortion?" She shook her head, saddened to realize her son could not see how wrong his father had been. "The O'Dea family's only claim to that treasure is that they helped to steal it, kept it from generations of its rightful owners, then demanded a piece of it as reward."

"'Tis true, Devin," Cameron said. "Our family's part in this is far from noble. That's why I insisted the gold had to go back." He turned to Michael. "I knew nothing of the dowry or your family's real claim on the gold."

"Even if I'd told you, behaving as I was, you wouldn't have believed me—and you'd have been right not to." Michael looked at Fiona. "I'd lost my grounding. I cared more about that treasure and about giving Devin back some antiquated notion of family honor than I did about doing what was right, what was Christian."

He put his hand on Cameron's shoulder. "If I had gotten the gold then, I fear I'd have lost much more than honor, much more than a hundred-year-old dowry."

"But you said it would only take one coin to prove your claim, Uncle Mike. With one of the original coins you can open the box and have the treasure." Devin slid off the bed and dug into his pocket. His voice came like that of a sad little boy. "What about this? I have a coin."

Michael looked to Cameron.

Cameron held up his hands. "As I've said, it's nothing to do with me, and I want nothing to do with it. I came here tonight to find the truth, and that I've done."

Michael glanced at the small, notched-edge coin in Devin's hand. "As for me, my heart is no longer in this. It's cost me a great deal to learn what I should have known so long ago when I first gave my life over to the Lord. But now I know where my treasure is, Fiona: it is first with the Lord and next with you."

Hearing his words strengthened Fiona in a way she had not expected. Now she knew that no matter what came their way, loving and being loved by this godly man was all she really wanted.

"I still don't see why you can't have your faith and the coins too, Uncle Mike."

Michael did not take his eyes from Fiona as he answered Devin. "I could—now. But before I was trying to serve two masters."

Devin frowned.

Cameron took one step to the nightstand, pulled open the drawer, and lifted out a Bible, which he handed to the boy. "Matthew 6, about two-thirds of the way through the chapter. The verse begins, 'No one can serve two masters.'"

Devin half groaned, half sighed, but he flipped through the pages and began to read aloud: "'No one can serve two masters. Either he will hate the one and love the other, or he will be devoted to the one and despise the other. You cannot serve both God and Money.'" He closed the book and looked up at Fiona, the coin still in his fisted hand. "I wasn't going to do that, Mom, honest."

"No one *intends* to do it, son." Michael never took his eyes off Fiona.

"But 'tis an easy trap to fall into," she said, as much to the man she loved as to her son. She took one step forward. "I know that at times I have put my work, my desire to succeed, to gain notice and be promoted, above my desire to seek God's will." She pulled in a deep breath to bolster her courage, then held out her hand to Michael. "I can't tell you how angry I felt, how cheated by God that you were rewarded with that promotion and I wasn't."

Michael opened his mouth to say something, but Devin grunted his discontent and spoke instead. "I still don't see why we can't just open the box, get the proof, and collect the coins!"

"You want some of those coins so badly, son?" Michael reached into his back pocket, pulled out his wallet, and fished out the tissue-wrapped cross necklace. "Take these."

Devin glared at Michael, ignoring the offering.

"What's that?" Cameron asked.

"Just something I made," Michael muttered. He unwrapped the tissue paper to reveal the shining gold. As he folded back the paper, a small, rectangular card somersaulted to the floor.

Michael handed Cameron the cross, then bent to retrieve the business card he'd been given at the craft fair.

"This is beautiful, Michael." Cameron held up the cross so the light played over the coins. "If I gave you the coin I was given as a reward, could I convince you to make one for me to give to Julia?"

"I could probably design a small one with one coin. That one took two, though, so it wouldn't be exactly the—"

"Here, take this one."

Fiona jerked her head up, expecting to find Devin volunteering the very cross Michael had designed for him. Instead, what she saw made her so proud of her child, she thought if the boy wouldn't have cringed with embarrassment, she'd have thrown her arms around him then and there.

Michael extended his fingers to take the coin in Devin's hand. "You know if I take this, son, and cut it and pound out the notches, we can't open the box with it."

Fiona bit her lower lip, knowing the remark was something of a test—a test she was anxious to have her son pass.

"I know." He let go of the coin, then reached to take the cross Michael had made for him. "But I was thinking about everything I've learned tonight, about Rose and Kerwin losing the money and starting over, and about how Owen got the O'Deas involved out of greed."

"Yes?" Fiona moved behind her son to help him fasten the cross around his neck.

"And about how Grandpa and Dad would have taken the money they believed belonged to the O'Dea family."

"But none of it does," Cameron interjected.

Devin nodded. "I was also thinking about that verse—about serving two masters—and how Mom said trying for a promotion at work sometimes made her feel that way."

Fiona sighed.

"And I realized I was making too much of this gold stuff. You guys don't want it, and it's messed up a lot of lives already." He gave Michael a serious look. "I just don't see what good could come out of opening that box—or out of getting back that gold."

"Don't be so sure, son."

Fiona tensed, unable to believe she'd heard Michael right. But when she turned to look at him, she saw him holding up the business card from the craft fair. Her spirits lifted as her gaze went from the cross around her son's neck to the card, then to Michael's grinning face. "Michael, that's a terrific idea."

"And the perfect solution to so many of our problems," Michael said.

"What?" Devin asked. "What's the perfect solution?"

"Devin, my son, if you were to pick up that Bible and glance a bit farther down into Matthew 7, you might have your answer."

"I don't have to work this hard in Sunday school," the boy complained as Cameron picked up the book and held it out to him.

Fiona, realizing that this message was as much for her as for her son, took the Bible from Cameron's hands. The thin pages slipped through her fingers until she found Matthew 7.

She read silently the beginning of the chapter that warned about not judging—worrying about the speck in another's eye while disregarding the plank in your own. A twinge of conviction made Fiona shiver. She'd done just that with Michael;

she'd judged and been jealous of him, disregarding her own shortcomings.

She read on, finally speaking aloud when she reached verse 6. "'Do not give dogs what is sacred; do not throw your pearls to pigs.'"

"Or your gold," Cameron added.

"Or even a job."

"What are you guys talking about?" Devin asked impatiently.

"We're just noting that if this gold had been given to us before we got our hearts right with God, it would have been like casting pearls before swine," Michael said.

"The same with the job promotion I have so wanted. If I had gotten it without realizing how misplaced my desire was, well...I know now I'll be fine whether I get it or not. My trust is where it belongs—not in my boss or in my own abilities but in my Lord."

Michael put his hand on her shoulder. "Read on."

She glanced down at verse 7, and it spoke directly to her heart. "'Ask and it will be given to you; seek and you will find; knock and the door will be opened to you.'"

"If you're ready now, Fiona, I think it's time we did just that," Michael said.

Devin groaned his frustration again. "Can't someone tell me what all this means in plain ol' English?"

"It means, son," Michael said with a broad grin, "that we've just found a way for me to reclaim Rose's dowry, use my talents, serve the Lord, and get your mother the promotion she's earned—all at the same time."

S i x t e e n

ose and Kerwin's marriage contract, with details of how
he was to receive the dowry; a note written by Kerwin; a
gold coin that matched the one taken from the cache
Cameron found and then returned; and a small, unremarkable
tool used by any metalsmith or jeweler, that Kerwin had
described in the note as his 'wee bit of insurance' to get the gold
that was his due. That's what we found in the silver box."
Michael leaned back against the counter at Gadabout Gifts.

"After that it was just a matter of Cameron making use of
his international contacts, a verification of the document, and,
after that, the gold coins," Fiona said.

"What an amazing story." Gadberry patted his stomach and
pursed his lips. "And you say this Cameron fellow has moved
to Cincinnati to do some kind of charity work?"

"He's going to run a shelter to keep women and children
from going homeless," Fiona said, proud as she could be of her
brother-in-law's new position.

"I didn't realize being in Interpol prepared you for that kind
of thing," Gadberry said with a chuckle.

"Mind you, he has an impressive work record and a heart
after God," Michael said. "And it doesn't hurt that his fund-
raising efforts with St. Patrick's Homeless Shelter impressed
powerful individuals and corporations alike."

"Oh, I see. Well then, that does make sense. But why would
such a man want to live in our lovely city when he could have
the world?"

"He met a lady." Fiona smiled at the thought of her brother-in-law finally finding a good Christian woman after avoiding romance for so long.

"Ah." Gadberry nodded slowly. "Yes, that happens."

"Yes." Michael inched nearer to Fiona until she could feel his breath stir her hair. "Yes, that does happen, thank the Lord."

"Still, I wish this whole gold business had a happier ending for me, Shaughnessy." Gadberry clasped his stubby fingers over his belly. "I really don't want to accept your resignation just when I had embraced the notion of someone else taking over the import buying."

Michael straightened away from Fiona, a new seriousness on his face. "See, now, that's not something you have to give up on, Mr.—"

"Michael, please." Fiona pressed the back of her hand against his chest and stepped forward. "If you don't mind, the last time you tried to speak for me on this matter, it didn't exactly turn out the way you'd planned."

His muffled chuckle brought a smile to her lips. If this whole adventure with the gold had taught her anything, it was that faith was not simply shown in prayer, but also in action. She had prayed for this chance, but until this very moment had done almost nothing to bring it about. She had wanted Mr. Gadberry to *give* her the job, but she had thought it showed a lack of faith to ask for it. *Ask and it will be given to you.*

She cleared her throat and squared her shoulders, glad she'd worn her very bright blue but professionally tailored suit today. "Mr. Gadberry, I have been a good and valued employee for some time now, wouldn't you say?"

"Why, yes, my dear, I don't know how I could run the shop without your help."

"I know every aspect of the day-to-day business from open to close, to ordering, stocking, and delivery."

"Indeed you do, dear."

"Then why, when you became convinced to allow someone else to handle a portion of the import ordering, did you skip right over me and choose Michael? When I was clearly the more qualified candidate?"

"We-ell..." His cheeks bulged as he blustered for a response.

"Are you in some way dissatisfied with the work I've done for you?"

"Oh, no, my dear, it's just that—"

"Do you not trust me to do a good job, to find the best bargains, to select the kinds of things our customers would favor?"

"No, no, and again no, but—"

"Then—and I have to ask this—is it because I'm a woman that you've never wanted to offer me a promotion?"

"Absolutely not." He flapped both hands in the air, palms out as though he were putting out an invisible fire. "No, no, Fiona, it has nothing to do with—"

"Then why haven't you promoted me, trusted me with more responsibility, or given me a decent raise in all this time?"

He batted his eyes, his face as red and round as a tomato, and choked out a deep but raspy laugh. "Because, my dear, you never asked."

"Oh."

To his credit, Michael did not join in Gadberry's laughter, even though Fiona herself felt a smile tugging at her lips as she called forth her most polished tone and said, "Well, then, Mr. Gadberry, I would very much like to have the job as your assistant in import buying for the shop."

"I'll give you the job on one condition."

Fiona folded her arms, suspicious of what the man might have in mind. "What condition?"

"Nothing difficult, my dear. I just want you to answer one question."

Her thoughts flew back over everything she had learned about the business—how to place orders, how to track inventory, all the tiny tidbits she had picked up along the way that he might try to trip her up on. She unfolded her arms, glanced at Michael for moral support, then lifted her chin. "All right. What's your question?"

He squinted at her, his face the picture of bulldog concentration. "What jeweler's tool was in that little silver box, and how did Kerwin think it could provide insurance to prove the coins were the ones given to him as Rose's dowry?"

Both Michael and Fiona burst out laughing. When they had grown serious again, Michael touched Fiona on the back and gestured toward the tool kit he'd brought with a sample of his work to show Gadberry. "May I?" he asked.

"By all means."

Michael took out a small tool that looked like an old, wooden-handled screwdriver, only with a fine, chiseled point. "This is what Kerwin had in the box."

Fiona took the tool and the coin that Michael held in his hand. She held up the thick coin for Gadberry's inspection. "You see these funny little notches spaced just so along the rim of the coin?"

"Yes."

"Well, none of us paid any particular attention to them, not knowing what this type of old coin *should* look like—until we opened the box," she explained.

"In his notes, my great-grandfather Kerwin had traced onto the paper one coin the way it was when it was given to him.

Then he wrote in detail what he had done to transform each and every coin in the dowry so they could be readily identified as his rightful property."

"The notches?" Gadberry asked.

"Made by this." Fiona held up the tool, then fit it exactly into the narrow but deep slot in the coin's edge. "See?"

"Well, I'll be." Gadberry chuckled. "Quite ingenious of your great-grandfather, I have to say, Shaughnessy."

Fiona arched one eyebrow. "Does this mean I've got the job, sir?"

"It does indeed, my dear." He gave her hand a firm, pumping handshake to seal the arrangement, then turned to Michael and shook his hand as well. "And the best of luck to you, too, my boy, in your new endeavor. You've got a good helping of your great-grandfather's adeptness, you have, in starting up a business making pieces of jewelry out of those old coins."

"I'll design other pieces as well, Mr. Gadberry. Ones without the coins. I already have a list of people who are interested in commissioning rings."

"And buying them through Gadabout Gifts?" Gadberry rubbed his hands together.

Michael fixed his twinkling gaze on Fiona. "That's something I'll have to take up with your new buyer, sir."

Even when Gadberry whacked him a solid slap on the back, Michael never looked away from her.

"You do that, Shaughnessy, you do that. Now, I'm off to an estate sale. Heard tell this place has got an amazing collection of unopened vintage cereal boxes!"

Fiona pressed her lips together to keep from laughing at her boss's enthusiasm for truly unique collectibles.

Michael gave her a wink.

Gadberry lumbered toward the door, calling to Fiona, "You

get this man under contractual obligation, my dear, and that's an order."

"Yes, sir," she whispered, her eyes on the man she loved, her heart filled with joy.

As Gadberry disappeared through the back door, Michael reached for Fiona and pulled her close.

She went to him happily.

When she was in the warm circle of his arms, he murmured, "Name the time and day, Fiona. I'm ready and willing for us to have that 'contractual obligation' whenever you say."

"Michael, please." She wet her lips, heat sweeping up over her cheeks at his forwardness. "It's just too soon. Don't you think you're moving a little fast?"

"Hmm, let's see." He tipped his head to one side. "We've known one another all our lives; we had our first date, oh, probably close to seventeen years ago; I've been like a father to your son since he lost his own dad. Now I have the outright nerve to suggest we do something rash, like rush into the marriage we both agreed to a mere fifteen years ago. What was I thinking?"

He bent his head low, his mouth brushing hers to show her exactly what he was thinking.

Fiona smiled and gave herself over to the sweet kiss, and to the idea that soon enough, after all these years, she would marry Michael Shaughnessy at last.

E p i l o g u e

THREE YEARS LATER

Happy Birthday to yoo-ou."

"Mom, please! Your singing is curdling my cake frosting!"

Devin yelped as Fiona retaliated by swiping her finger through the frosting and planting a dollop on his nose.

Michael laughed. How grand his life had become, he thought. How rich. How full.

Devin had grown into a thoughtful, happy teenager, made all the more cheerful today by the fact that he had just gotten his driver's license. His grades, along with his whole attitude, had vastly improved, although both still suffered setbacks from time to time.

Fiona had become so good at her job that Gadberry had gone into semiretirement. They'd hired a full-time sales staff, and Fiona had taken over buying everything but the antiques and collectibles, the latter of which, thankfully, made up a much smaller portion of the inventory than before. Thanks to her hard work making trustworthy contacts, and with the help of the Internet, she now did most of her work from the computer at home.

Michael's business had prospered more than he could have imagined. And married life agreed with him wonderfully well. God had blessed him with more than he deserved, more than any earthly treasure could ever have provided.

"Oh-ooh."

"Mom, I told you you could stop singing," Devin said, grinning as he wiped the white frosting from the tip of his nose.

"That wasn't singing, young man. That was—oh-oh-ohhh."

"Oh, no. It's not—" Michael rushed to his wife's side. "Is it time?"

His very pregnant wife could only nod, her knees buckling as she grasped at his arm for support.

"This is it, everybody," Michael announced to the family gathered around the kitchen table in their new home. "Okay, Fiona, remember what we learned about breathing. Take a deep, cleansing breath and we'll get through this with a minimum of discomfort."

His dear, loving wife gave him a withering glare. "We'll talk discomfort after this is—oh-oh-over."

"Devin, get your mother's suitcase." Cameron stood, his chair clattering backward. He dipped into his jeans pocket to pull out a heavy key chain. "Get her into my car, Michael. I'll drive."

"Cameron, honey, you can't take her in our car." Julia Reed O'Dea, Cameron's wife of two years, rose from the table as well. "We haven't got room, what with Neal Michael's car seat and all his things in the backseat."

She put her hand on the back of the high chair where their nine-month-old son sat whacking a plastic baby spoon against a paper plate. "Besides, I promised Craig that I'd spell him at the shelter for a while this afternoon so he can go with his wife to her doctor's appointment. They're going to hear the baby's heartbeat today, and he'd die if he missed that."

"Then I'll drive your car," Cameron said to Michael, who was already helping Fiona toward the door.

"If you go with them, who's going to watch Neal Michael when I go in to work for Craig?" Julia took the spoon from her

216

green-eyed terror of a boy and shook it at her husband, smiling. "Not to mention that I would like to be there for Fiona, just like she was for me when I struggled through twenty-two hours of hard labor."

"Don't you go pulling the 'hard labor' card on me now, sweet Julia." He could hardly contain his proud grin for his feisty wife and for the joy that her labor had produced. "I'll be glad to take care of Neal Michael. But right now we have to get Fiona to the hospital. This isn't her first child, and she probably won't have the luxury of a long labor—"

"Luxury?" Julia sputtered. Then a smile that reached all the way to the depths of her eyes lit her face. "Oh, am I ever going to get a lot of mileage out of *that* remark, mister."

Fiona made a soft sound as she pulled in a long breath, then held it, just as she'd been taught in her birthing class.

Cameron cast her a worried glance. "Speaking of mileage, let's put some on my car—now."

Julia hurried forward. "Maybe I should drive Fiona and Michael, and you can—"

"I can drive them." Cameron pushed her hair back off her shoulder. "You can come down to the hospital later in our car, and I'll—"

"We won't be *at* the hospital later if we don't get moving now," Fiona said through clenched teeth.

Neal Michael howled out a protest at being left alone at the table, and both his parents turned to check on him.

"Here's Mom's bag." Devin ran into the room, his face flushed. "What do you want me to do with it?"

"Bring it with you," Michael ordered.

"What?" the boy squawked.

Michael dug out his car keys and tossed them to his stepson. "What do you think, son? Can you get your mom and me to the hospital before you become a brother?"

"Yes, sir!"

"Michael! I don't think—whooo-ooh."

"You don't need to think about this. Devin will do fine."

"But it's his first day as a licensed dri-i-i—"

"I told you I'd be driving my first day, Mom." Devin grinned.

"That hasn't been decided yet," Fiona said, then moaned.

"Enough talk!" Michael shouted.

Everyone stopped and stared at him. He used the sudden silence to bark out orders.

"You—breathe," he said, taking his wife's arm. Then he pointed to Devin. "You—drive."

"Let's go, Mom." Devin took Fiona by the other arm, and together they escorted her out the front door.

"Call the doctor, Julia," Michael called out before the door closed. "Tell him we're on our way."

At 4:41 that afternoon, Erin Rose Shaughnessy was born. Her parents, brother, and doting aunt and uncle all agreed that there was no greater treasure on earth than the joy of a child, the love of family, and the gift of God's salvation.

Dear Reader,

Every story has two sides, and when writing a romance, one tends to think of those two sides as being "his" and "hers." When the legacy of the gold coins, a character named Fiona (whom I really liked), and the enigmatic Michael Shaughnessy all took shape in *Irish Eyes,* I realized that this story had a his and hers and *another* his and hers. And so I decided to tell the story of Michael and Fiona in *Irish Rogue.*

I found the research in Irish crafts and culture fascinating and fun. This really enabled me to add a wonderful texture to the characters. And, as usual when I work on a Palisades book, the writing research was only a small part of what I learned. As the characters grow and face the challenges of living their faith, I find I, too, must consider my own walk.

It is my hope that in reading *Irish Rogue,* or any of my books, that you come away with not just something to dream about (fun and adventure and so on), but that you also have something to think about.

Blessings!

Write to Annie Jones
c/o Palisades
Multnomah Publishers, Inc.
P.O. Box 1720
Sisters, Oregon 97759

Palisades...Pure Romance

⌐ Palisades ⌐

Reunion, Karen Ball
Refuge, Lisa Tawn Bergren
Torchlight, Lisa Tawn Bergren
Treasure, Lisa Tawn Bergren
Chosen, Lisa Tawn Bergren
Firestorm, Lisa Tawn Bergren
Surrender, Lynn Bulock
Wise Man's House, Melody Carlson
Heartland Skies, Melody Carlson (March 1998)
Cherish, Constance Colson
Chase the Dream, Constance Colson
Angel Valley, Peggy Darty
Sundance, Peggy Darty
Moonglow, Peggy Darty
Promises, Peggy Darty
Memories, Peggy Darty (May 1998)
Remembering the Roses, Marion Duckworth (June 1998)
Love Song, Sharon Gillenwater
Antiques, Sharon Gillenwater
Texas Tender, Sharon Gillenwater
Secrets, Robin Jones Gunn
Whispers, Robin Jones Gunn
Echoes, Robin Jones Gunn
Sunsets, Robin Jones Gunn
Clouds, Robin Jones Gunn
Waterfalls, Robin Jones Gunn (February 1998)
Coming Home, Barbara Jean Hicks
Snow Swan, Barbara Jean Hicks
China Doll, Barbara Jean Hicks (June 1998)
Angel in the Senate, Kristen Johnson Ingram (March 1998)
Irish Eyes, Annie Jones

Father by Faith, Annie Jones
Irish Rogue, Annie Jones
Glory, Marilyn Kok
Sierra, Shari MacDonald
Forget-Me-Not, Shari MacDonald
Diamonds, Shari MacDonald
Stardust, Shari MacDonald
Westward, Amanda MacLean
Stonehaven, Amanda MacLean
Everlasting, Amanda MacLean
Kingdom Come, Amanda MacLean
Betrayed, Lorena McCourtney
Escape, Lorena McCourtney
Dear Silver, Lorena McCourtney
Forgotten, Lorena McCourtney (February 1998)
Enough! Gayle Roper
The Key, Gayle Roper (April 1998)
Voyage, Elaine Schulte

— ANTHOLOGIES —

A Christmas Joy, Darty, Gillenwater, MacLean
Mistletoe, Ball, Hicks, McCourtney
A Mother's Love, Bergren, Colson, MacLean
Silver Bells, Bergren, Krause, MacDonald
Heart's Delight, Ball, Hicks, Noble
Fools for Love, Ball, Brooks, Jones (March 1998)